PRAYER

BEING DILIGENT TO ENTER INTO HIS REST

Author of *Fasting* and *Revealing God*

MICHAEL DOW

BURNING ONES
PUBLISHING

DEDICATION

To all of you who have gotten a glimpse of this wonderful lover, this great King, and have been completely ravished by the romance continually flowing out of His heart towards you. To all of those who have realized that even in the small glimpse you may feel you have caught of Him, that with the little you have seen, He is worthy for you to give Him everything.

This is for you. The one trying to give Him everything. To the one giving it your all. Not in some weird way of striving, but by allowing Him to occupy a greater space in the place of your yes to Him. To the one that is yielding and allowing the softening of your heart toward Him, this is for you.

May you be completely overwhelmed by this life of joyous devotion unto the only One that is worthy. He is worthy of our attention. He is worthy of our affection. He is worthy of our lives.

May He, by His Spirit, possess such a people in the earth. May He raise up lovers, overwhelmed by His nearness, praying and contending with their lives for His Kingdom to come on the earth as it is in Heaven. This is our moment. This is your life.

May you be infused with His life to enter into His rest!

TABLE OF CONTENTS

ACKNOWLEDGMENTS

To my wife, Anna, and my children, Ariyah, Josiah, Emma, and Isaiah, I love you with all of my heart. Outside of Jesus, you are my greatest joy. Thank you for the strength you provide to my life by graciously loving me and cheering me on.

Thank you to our Burning Ones team. Your faithfulness to challenge me because of what you see in and on my life is a constant reminder to me of God's faithfulness.

Thank you to Kathy Curtis, who always labors alongside of me in these projects with excellence, diligence, and love. Your work over the years to assist with all of these books has been a great help from the Lord. I look forward to many more together, Lord willing.

Thank you to my friend, my dear brother, Omar Galarza, for a cover design that absolutely hit the mark. Your creativity is a gift and I am grateful for your contribution to this project.

Thank you to all of you who over the years have impacted my heart and life in a way that challenged and provoked me to realize that there was a deeper place in the well to immerse my life. Your life of prayer has affected the content in the pages that follow.

PRELUDE

"The apostles gathered to Jesus and told Him all things, both what they had done and what they had taught. And He said to them, 'Come away by yourselves to a deserted place and rest a while.' "[1]

Consider the scenario in the verse above. The disciples, or the apostles, as they are described in the text in Mark's gospel, have come to gather with Jesus. In coming to gather with Him they begin to report all they have accomplished. Their productivity is what seems to be paramount. The centerpiece of conversation is all of the work they have been able to do. They are gathering together in the presence of Jesus, face-to-face, and their attention is on their own

---

[1] Mark 6:31, NKJV

accomplishments and abilities. They have come to Him, but their focus doesn't seem to just simply be on Him. In the place of His presence and being with Him they are more concerned with themselves—what they are able to do and bring to Him. This is a problem. Yet it is a problem that they don't yet recognize.

In response to all of the excitement with what they are able to bring to Jesus, He responds to them in a way that seems a little odd. Jesus immediately takes inventory of the situation and instead of joining in and rejoicing with them in their excitement, He calls them away with Him by themselves to a solitary place so that they can rest for a while. Huh? Did I miss something here? They had been busy. They had been out ministering and doing the work, in power and with incredible results. It's not that the activity isn't important to Jesus; I'm sure He was rejoicing with them. However, there is something that is more important to Him than their productivity and this is what He is getting to. He cares more about them than what they can do for Him or bring to Him.

Jesus called them away with Him to a secluded place to rest. We have to actually see Jesus' invitation here and not just passively overlook it. In fact, it is more than an invitation; it is a prescription. Prescriptions are typically issued after a diagnosis has been determined. We are most familiar with prescriptions used in medical terms, for medication. Only Jesus isn't trying to medicate them; His desire is to heal them. The only issue for them, and for most, is that they have no idea what they need to be healed from.

Jesus hurdles the conversational front of productivity that they bring to Him and He dives right into the heart of the matter. Behind their celebration of things lingers an issue that Jesus directly confronts by His invitation to come away. The issue is that they are in His presence and they are more aware of and consumed by the things they bring to Him rather than Jesus Himself. Their accomplishments and revelations have become their joyful offering to Jesus. I know this doesn't initially sound like a big deal, but the implications of overlooking this run deep and wide within the heart and the attentions thereof.

Our hearts get cluttered so easily. When our hearts get cluttered our attention begins to diversify. In response to the cluttering of the heart and the diverting of attention, Jesus offers Himself. His offering is Himself. Come away with Me, by yourself, for a while, and rest. Jesus offers Himself for He knows that He is all that we need. There is no other remedy. The desperate need of the heart and life is Jesus. And He knows that in order to recalibrate their hearts He must get them to come away with Him, to rest. In order to realign them He offers them rest in Him.

Jesus knows that rest both realigns and recalibrates our hearts.

The anchor of our hearts must be plunged deeply and rooted securely into the person of Jesus. If we aren't careful the heart so easily gets entertained and entangled with things and stuff. Then before we know it, much about us has changed.

The anchor of our hearts must be plunged deeply and rooted securely into the person of Jesus.

When we lose simplicity in Jesus our conversation changes. When the simple beauty of rest in Jesus gets disrupted, so do the things we talk about, and pray about. When our hearts' alignment and attentiveness shift, there is a tendency to find reports, things, and stuff to be of greater concern than just enjoying being with Him. The way that we attempt to generate a restful satisfaction morphs when we aren't coming to Him for only Him and allowing Him alone to be our all and in Him finding our needed rest.

Much of life is attempting to get you to find your rest in something or someone other than Jesus. There are even weapons formed by design against you, attempting to completely demolish your quality of life by luring you into the restlessness that comes by defining your life by your accomplishments and abilities. But your rest is not to be in your accomplishments and abilities. This isn't where the anchor goes. Jesus is our rest. In Him we truly find rest. Our hearts were made to find their rest in Him, and this is why He offers Himself.

Just as He said to the apostles that day, He says to you, "Come away with Me. Away from all of the things that are vying for your attention. Away from all of the things that tend to dominate the conversation. Away from all of the distractors and disruptors. Away to find your rest in Me. Away to revive your restful confidence in Me. Away to find your joyful contentment in Me. Come away. Come away with Me, to a secluded place for a while; it's time."

INTRODUCTION

Hello, and greetings to you in Jesus' name. I am thankful to the Lord to be able to meet you this way. In fact, the Lord has spoken to my heart about you. I believe this is a setup, a setup of a divine nature; some would call it a divine appointment; a moment that issues out of a divine desire. Just know this, you are on God's heart. He thinks about you constantly with a burning jealousy that is set for you and only you. This burning desire, I believe, brought you to this moment where our lives cross paths in the form of this book.

I think it's incredibly important that I share my goal with you upfront, right here in the beginning of what is sure to be an adventure as we continue into the content found in the pages that follow in this book. My goal is simple: to share about prayer. However, prayer is a very broad and deep subject matter, so I will make it much more definite than that.

I feel a very real responsibility to share on a specific, narrow, you could say, slant in the place, or conversation, of prayer. My slant is this: the motivations of the heart and how they affect rest. You may pray frequently. You may pray fervently. You may even pray, as you think currently, very freely. However, it will be our goal throughout the rest of this book to identify and unravel the motivations that have filled your heart and how they affect your life in prayer.

Motivation doesn't just simply inform us on *what* you are doing; it provides great insight into *why* you may be doing it. This book will deal very specifically with the *why* you do all that you do. It may or may not sound like a great need for you to tackle such a subject matter, but I beg to differ, obviously. I am writing a book about it.

This book will be a conversation that deals with the importance of rest in your life. Rest is critically important because it affects everything about you. Rest is not a peripheral issue. Rest is not some supplemental thing in life that if we happen to ever encounter it, then it should be perceived as a bonus. Rest is a foundation. Rest is a hinge. Rest is a way. Rest is a game changer. Let's say simply, for now, that rest directly affects your motivations.

Rest affects more than just your motivations, but for the overall point we are seeking to build, we will say, rest definitely and very directly affects your motivations. Much of what you do, and do not do, is informed and affected by whether or not you are at rest. In many instances the motivations of our hearts are influenced by rest or restlessness. And the sad part for some is that they are unable to identify which is which.

We have to give a proper working definition to rest; otherwise things will get a little blurry moving forward. We will define rest in this way—*a freedom that empowers innocence*. Rest cannot simply be perceived as an absence of activity. I understand that at times it can be, but only when we are talking about the physicality of activity and how that connects to rest. But rest is not only defined by your activity. We must see rest as best defined by the condition of your heart.

Rest cannot be limited to activity alone, because you can have no movement, nothing going on at all, and still not be at rest. Rest is not limited to the activity that is done on the outside, meaning externally. Rest directly deals with and brings confrontation to the activity that is happening on the inside, meaning internally.

Again, you can have nothing happening and still not be at rest. Or, you can have a lot going on, be extremely busy, and be completely at rest. Rest isn't limited to activities because it challenges and reveals motivations. The issue isn't simply *what* you are doing, but the motive as to *why* you may be doing it. It is necessary to bring to light the other definitions of rest so that they will help to provide context to our conversation.

In addition to a lack of activity or movement, rest can be defined as a refreshing ease; relief or freedom, especially from anything that wearies, troubles, or disturbs; mental or spiritual calm. This diversifies our understanding of rest a little bit. Anything that isn't operating in or being birthed out of ease is in need of rest. Please take note, I didn't say easy, I said ease; the two are very different. You can have ease when something isn't necessarily easy. Ease flows out of rest.

Anything that is not operating from or being birthed out of freedom is in need of rest. Anything that has been a disruption to spiritual calm, by way of producing weariness, troubles, and disturbances, is in desperate need of rest.

Rest is vitally important in the life of a believer, especially in the place of prayer. Rest is important, and desperately needed, because I don't believe you can truly be free or honest until you are at rest. Many times, we are motivated and animated by things that we are simply unaware of—rest reveals the power of these influencers in our hearts. Many times we don't understand what is actually influencing us until we are at rest. Rest, or a lack of rest, affects your actions, your interactions, your language, your appetite, and more. It is of grave importance that we be aware of what is actually happening in our hearts.

The writer of Hebrews brings encouragement to our hearts about rest with these words, "Be diligent to enter into His rest..."[2] Diligence? What does diligence have to do with rest? And wouldn't diligence imply the opposite of an attempt to rest? I'm glad you asked. Diligence implies a constant effort to accomplish something. Diligence speaks to something that is done or pursued with persevering attentiveness. Really, diligence speaks of work, labor.

The encouragement we find from the writer of Hebrews provokes us to understand that entering into His rest may take work. In fact, another translation words it this way, which provides a little bit of a clearer picture of what we mean, "Let us labor therefore to enter into that rest..."[3] And yet another translation has it this way, "Let us therefore strive to enter that rest..."[4] These other translations help to bring greater clarity to the task at hand with entering into rest.

---

[2] Heb 4:11, NASB
[3] Heb 4:11, KJV
[4] Heb 4:11, ESV

Getting into rest will require diligence. Fighting to get into rest will require perseverance. Getting into and remaining at a place of rest will require striving. Although these words seem to paint a picture that is radically opposite than our normal working definition of rest, it is important to hold them in the light of the motivations of our hearts and not just the activity of our hands and life.

In the journey of writing this book I have had to take a fresh look at the motivations of my own heart. I have been greatly challenged and encouraged as the processing of my heart has been laid bare before the Lord. There is a great beauty in having your heart filleted wide open by the Holy Spirit. It is here, in the place of intimate exposure and vulnerability before the Lord, that we have the potential to experience powerful transformation.

The motivations of the heart that influence the posture from which we pray will be the target, and not so much just the action of prayer itself. You are being influenced right now. The goal of our time together will be to sift through the matters of the heart to find out by what.

I am praying for you. I believe that if you are ready, God will, by His Spirit, fillet your heart wide open. It is greatly needed. Let the Lord put His finger on things in you that motivate you. Allow the Lord, by

His Spirit, to speak to your heart. I honestly believe with all of my heart that what lies ahead of you could change you forever.

With all of that said, dear lover of Jesus, let us be diligent to enter into His rest!

CHAPTER 1
JESUS

God wants you to be at rest. God desires that your life be lived from a beautiful place of rest in Him. This was Jesus' invitation that He issued as He spoke to the crowd in Matthew chapter 11. Jesus said, "Come to Me, all of you who are weary and heavy burdened, and I will give you rest."[5] Jesus promised rest. Jesus promised rest by coming to Him.

In coming to Jesus, He has made it clear that He and He alone is able to bring rest to our hearts. What a tremendous invitation. What a beautiful promise. And it isn't a hollow invitation. Jesus' invitation is not one that is empty. He is able to fill it, and fill it to over-flowing. Why? Because He fills it with Himself. His offering wasn't solutions. It wasn't answers. It wasn't

---

[5] Matt 11:28, NASB

provision. It wasn't breakthrough. It was Himself. He said come to Me. I am more than enough. I am forever all that you need. In Me, come and find rest for your souls. Praise God!

Rest must be seen, understood, and experienced in the context of the person of Jesus.

We have to see rest as something that is found in Jesus and as something that continually issues out of Jesus. Rest must be seen, understood, and experienced in the context of the person of Jesus. For our purpose together, we will define rest this way: *a freedom that empowers innocence.*

You may be a little taken aback by the way we will define rest, but let me explain. Freedom can be defined as the state of being free, or at liberty, rather than being in confinement or under restraint. Innocence can be defined as simplicity or being without guile. Guile is another way to say crafty, or artful deception. So, what we are really saying is that rest can be defined as the simple liberty to be free from deception or manipulation.

It is much easier to be fully aligned with God's heart and desires when at rest. As we fully align our hearts and lives with God's heart, we can begin to understand the great need to pray for the fullness of His desires to be manifested in our lives and the earth. Prayers like "Your Kingdom Come" and "Your Will Be Done" flow freely and powerfully from a heart that is at rest. A life lived this way is something that Jesus demonstrated while He spent time among us on the earth. The life of Jesus was one fully aligned with God's heart and therefore able to manifest His desires through His life, but also and especially in the place of prayer.

Jesus stands in the midst of a crowd of people in John chapter 17 and He prays. He prays out loud, not for His own sake, because He already knows that He is intimately connected to His Father and that His prayers are heard. But rather He prays for the sake of those gathered around Him. He prays what He knows is on His Father's heart. He prays it boldly. He prays it beautifully. He prays it because He is completely preoccupied with His Father and His Father's desires.

Jesus doesn't have His own agenda, not even in the place of prayer. He is submitted to His Father, at rest, and free to fulfill the will of Him who sent Him. Jesus is able to pray what is on His Father's heart because He doesn't have some weird, manipulative goal in prayer or some ambitious desire that hasn't yet found the freedom that comes through rest. He isn't trying to be impressive; He desires to be obedient. He has no goal of pleasing people, only pleasing the heart of His Father. And all of this is directly influencing what and how He chooses to pray.

Jesus is able to pray simply and freely because He doesn't have a point to prove. He isn't praying to win His Father's favor; His heart is settled about all of this. The motivation of His heart is free from feeling He needs to prove something. This simple point is important, because, no matter how free you may think you are, you will never be completely free so long as you feel you have something to prove.

Your point to prove will always be the point that restricts your freedom rather than releasing it.

The person who has a point to prove will never be free. That point can be towards other people around you. That point can be towards yourself. That point can even be towards God. However, regardless of who you may be trying to prove something to, your point to prove will always be the point that restricts your freedom rather than releasing it.

Without getting too ahead of ourselves here, Jesus gives us a beautiful picture in John 17 of what is possible for us in the place of prayer. Jesus, as always, is our pattern. Jesus is our model. Jesus is our perfect example of what is possible for a man or woman walking the earth, filled with the Holy Spirit, totally surrendered to the Father, completely overwhelmed by His joyful love, and living fully alive from and out of that place. We shouldn't ever seek to settle for less than what Jesus has made available. This wasn't just something He lived as a demonstration; it was something He lived as an invitation, an invitation to the fullness of what is available!

What is available? Pulling Heaven into earth through prayer, that's what's available! This is one of the things that Jesus is demonstrating. Living in beautiful surrender to the Father, Jesus prays for His will to be done on the earth as it is in Heaven. Jesus understands that bound up in the heart of the Father is the desire to see the Kingdom fully manifested upon the earth, and as His Son, He joyfully bears that burden with Him in the place of prayer. And likewise, now, it is our joy and privilege as sons and daughters to join into this burden. As our lives join into joyful surrender to the Father, we can pray for Heaven to be released upon the earth through prayer.

As our lives join into joyful surrender to the Father, we can pray for Heaven to be released upon the earth through prayer.

Although this is available, we must consider that some have not entered into this joyful participation. Why wouldn't someone join in? Well, it becomes very difficult to pray for His Kingdom *to come* and His will *to be done* when we are hard set on seeking the accomplishment of our own will. It becomes hard to honestly pray for God's will to be done when we are bent on having things our way, especially if there is an ounce within us that would consider that His will may not be in harmony with what we are desiring through prayer.

The other things will never be able to wholly bring freedom to your life the way that rest in Jesus does. Jesus is and will forever be more than enough.

Our desires and God's desires are not always congruent with one another. This is one of the reasons we so desperately need rest. This is one of the reasons that our rest must be found in Jesus. Rest can seem to be found in many other things and places; however, all of these other things may seem to promise rest, but they will never be able to fully satisfy the soul of the weary life with rest. The other things may temporarily bring relief to the mind, or alleviate the pressure upon your heart, but they will never be able to wholly bring freedom to your life the way that rest in Jesus does.

Rest must be found in Jesus. He said come to Me. Instead of trying to come up with something, come to Me. This is the invitation. This will forever be the invitation. Come to Me, and I will give you rest. You may find a lot of other things along the way, but these other things are not the same as Jesus. The influence of these other things may temporarily seem to be sufficient, but they will never be enough. Jesus is and will forever be more than enough.

As we begin, let us begin by coming to Jesus. This is not just the beginning, as if to assume there will ever come a time when this is no longer applicable or desperately needed. Coming to Jesus is the beginning, it is the middle, it is the end, and He is the life that fills it all and holds it all together. He is glorious. Allow His preeminence to fill your heart and life as you come to Him to find His rest.

As we begin our journey, I would ask you to pray the following prayer. Just take a moment right now and turn all of your attention to Jesus, and say this as simply and as honestly as you know how:

Jesus, You are everything. I intentionally look away from every other thing and person right now and I look unto You. I need You to become everything to me. I abandon the pursuit of rest being found in other places and I respond to Your invitation; I come to You right now. I bring all of my heart to You. I need You; I need Your rest. Touch my heart and set me free, Lord. In the wonderful name of Jesus. Amen.

Let's continue our journey in the next chapter by talking about preoccupation.

CHAPTER 2
PREOCCUPATION

"I have set the Lord continually before me;
Because He is at my right hand, I will not be
shaken."[6]

Let's begin with defining what preoccupation means. I prefer to understand the definition of a word so that I can then interact with a specific word, or term, correctly. Definitions help to shed light, or give fuller meaning, when certain phrases are constructed, or ideas are formed. So then, preoccupation, or the state of being preoccupied, can simply be defined as being completely engrossed in thought; absorbed; previously occupied; taken; filled.

---

[6] Ps 16:8, NASB

The idea of being preoccupied means to be completely consumed. Or, more simply put, to not have any room. The picture that gets painted with the thought of using the word preoccupied is that there is a space that doesn't have any vacancy. There is a space that has been completely filled or overtaken to remove anything that might have been there or occupied it prior to. This is a powerful thought.

No vacancy means that you have been filled. Being filled means that you are completely absorbed, you are taken, you are filled to max capacity. Being filled to max capacity means that you don't have any room available for something else to be able to fit. I know this may seem a little redundant and extremely simple, yet it has very serious and beautiful implications when we apply it to the thought of what we are building here. Let's continue.

Preoccupation becomes a really big deal when we apply it to the matters of the heart. The preoccupations of the heart are a big deal when we consider how all of this affects rest. The preoccupations of the heart affect your day-to-day quality of life. They affect your day-to-day quality of life because it is here, in the preoccupations of the heart, that we find what moves us.

They move us to pray. They influence the things that we are moved to say, and the things that we don't say. They affect the way we are moved to believe and what we believe. The preoccupations of the heart become important if we consider the things that have influence in and upon our hearts and lives. Let's put it this way, preoccupation many times directly affects your intentions and your actions.

The preoccupations of the heart deal with what moves us. As you have given your life to Jesus and been filled with His Spirit, there is a wonderful promise to you to be able to live and walk in the power of the Holy Spirit. Galatians tells us that if we live by the Spirit, we are also to walk by the Spirit. Then, as we live and walk by the Spirit, we will not gratify our lustful, or fleshly, desires.[7]

There is great hope in Jesus in being filled with His Spirit to break the bondage of a lustful, fleshly life. This promise implies that we don't have to be moved by our fleshly desires. Our lives don't have to be governed by the things that are constantly tugging at our natural, or fleshly senses, and demanding a response or reaction.

We can remain settled regardless of what is happening to us or around us in life by way of

> **Preoccupation many times directly affects your intentions and your actions. The preoccupations of the heart deal with what moves us.**

---

[7] Gal 5:16, NASB

circumstantial evidence. We can remain calm. We can stay at rest. We can stay confident. Why? Because our promise of walking in the Spirit is valid in every season and situation. This promise doesn't wane because life can be shifty and unpredictable at times. Our flesh may have fickle tendencies, but our Spirit is steadfastly determined. In this we have great hope.

Having the Holy Spirit allows us to know the mind of Christ. We have real access to God's thoughts. By the Spirit we can know what God is saying about what we are facing, and anything that we may be going through. Knowing God's heart towards us and having the availability to His voice in and through His Word at all times in our life is what settles us and gives us confidence.

We want our hearts to become filled with His Word. We want to be preoccupied with the voice of God. We want to be preoccupied with the presence of God. This is your promise as one filled with His Spirit. This is the place you are to find your preoccupation. Your preoccupation is to be occupied by His presence and His voice.

There is a story in the Old Testament of a prophet named Elijah that provides for us a beautiful picture of why the preoccupations of the heart become so vitally important in the life of a believer. Let's jump right in. We will pick up this story in the book of 1 Kings chapter 17, verse number 1, "Now Elijah the Tishbite, who was of the settlers of Gilead, said to Ahab, 'As the Lord, the God of Israel lives, before whom I stand, surely there will be neither dew nor rain these years, except by my word.' "[8]

Elijah is a man that comes into the biblical narrative completely overwhelmed. He is not overwhelmed because he is impressed with Ahab; not at all. Elijah is overwhelmed by the preoccupations of his heart and the purpose that he knows his life has secured in the place of God's presence. Elijah is a man that is moved, just not by the natural influencing agents that seem to surround him. Elijah is preoccupied. He is a man that is under the influence. Elijah's life has been overtaken by things that he cannot necessarily see outwardly, yet they have become the governor of his life from an inward place. What is happening on the inside of Elijah is now affecting all of his movement and language that is coming out on the outside.

Elijah arrives because he must speak with Ahab. Although it seems that Elijah has come to speak *with* Ahab, it is better understood that Elijah knows he must speak *to* Ahab. He is speaking to Ahab, but also, he is speaking to the natural environment that surrounds

---

[8] 1 Kings 17:1, NASB

him. Elijah has not just come with a confrontation for the natural king, but also the natural order.

Elijah's influence is not fueled by a sense of being impressed with the king that stands before him, that being Ahab. Elijah's influence comes from the place in which he knows there is a King that he stands before. This is where the difference maker is found. Elijah's King has a place of council and Elijah knows that he has been granted access into this wonderful place of divine council. Elijah's King, before whom he stands, has a place of seeing and hearing. Elijah has seen, he has heard, and now he has come to declare.

In the book of Jeremiah, the prophet asks this question, "But who has stood in the council of the Lord, to see and to hear His word? Who has paid attention to His word and obeyed?"[9] Jeremiah also reveals to us that there is a place of council in which God dwells where His desires are revealed. This is the place from which Elijah has entered our story. It is from here that Elijah has found his preoccupation. It is from here too where we must find our preoccupation.

Elijah is up against impossible odds, yet he is unafraid. Elijah is going to declare something that he totally does not have the power to pull off in his own strength. It must require God fulfilling His word.

---

[9] Jer 23:18, CSB

Elijah knows he is completely dependent on God moving, yet he himself is unmoved. Elijah is opening up his mouth in confidence, believing that what he is declaring is something that originated in God's heart before it came crashing into his. He is able to declare boldly, for he knows that there is not some weird, ambitious desire tied into what he is declaring that points back to himself. He wants what God wants. He is free from agenda. If we see it clearly and understand what is happening, this is all so incredibly beautiful.

Elijah shows up and releases a word that it will not rain until he says so. Seriously? You either have to be a complete lunatic or be totally convinced, and convicted, that something you have heard must be released in order to see it come to pass. Elijah is obviously of the latter company. He declares that it will not rain, and then he disappears.

It is important to point out that the Bible says it didn't rain from that point on for the next three-and-a-half years. Elijah was faithful to release what he knew was in his heart. His heart didn't waiver in the moment of opportunity because of the pressure of the situation that was forming around him. Even at the cost of penalty for his obedience, he prophesied!

Elijah is a man that is preoccupied with the presence of God and the word of the Lord. The preoccupations of his heart are consumed by the presence of a real God that he knows he has access to, that he literally stands before, and a word that is now burning in his bones. The preoccupations of Elijah's heart have not been infected. Doubt, fear, anxiety, and all the more, have not found vacancy in the heart of Elijah. Because he is preoccupied these other intruders and influencers may be speaking, but they have not found a space in order to begin residing.

Being preoccupied doesn't by any means suggest that these other intruders, these infections of sorts, will not attempt to come and find a place. It doesn't mean that just because you know you walk in God's presence or know what He is saying, that it will by default just eliminate these other void fillers. It is a fight. It requires an intentional yielding to the Spirit. We will see this fight play out later on in Elijah's life. It won't end the way that you may think, but it's okay.

Elijah is fully preoccupied with what he knows God is saying. So much so that it no longer matters for him to "go show himself" or to "go hide himself." He is free from personal agenda that would motivate him to occupy the place of God's council only when there seemed to be a personal interest or individualized benefit directed toward himself. Elijah just wants whatever it is that he knows God wants. His life has become moved solely by what he receives in the place of God's council. Elijah is a man moved only by God's presence and voice.

Elijah stands before the Lord in the place of His council. This place of council has become a powerful reality that informs and influences all of his life. So, whether in front of Ahab, the brook, the widow woman, the dead boy, Mt. Carmel, or awaiting the cloud the size of the man's hand, Elijah is no longer simply informed and influenced by what he sees naturally, and this is possible because of how his preoccupation has been taken up with God Himself. Elijah may be informed by what he sees, but he is also moved by the council in which he stands. Those who have been overtaken by God's influence shall not be taken under by the circumstantial evidence of the world.

Those who have been overtaken by God's influence shall not be taken under by the circumstantial evidence of the world.

However, we have an account later in the life of Elijah that should be somewhat startling to us, an episode that should challenge us and provide the necessary fuel for us to consistently cling to the Lord in a greater way. The Bible tells us about a moment where Elijah becomes moved by something else, another presence and voice, a moment where his preoccupation would shift.

First Kings chapter 19 opens with an interesting description for the source of this shift in the life of Elijah. We will share the details quickly to create a proper context. Context is important; it helps to provide the canvas upon which God will paint our point here.

Ahab tells Jezebel, his wife, of all God is doing in and with the life of Elijah. Jezebel isn't happy with the testimony that is coming out of the prophet's life, the powerful way God is using him. Jezebel is offended by the man that is consumed by God's voice and acting on it. She is so offended that she decides to send a messenger to Elijah to inform him that she intends to kill him and will do everything in her power in order to see that desire fulfilled. No big deal, right? Surely, after all that Elijah has been through up until this point in his life, this won't be able to detour him, right? Wrong. In fact, very wrong.

There is a fascinating progression that happens in the life of Elijah at this point. Elijah receives the message from Jezebel's messenger. Elijah processes what Jezebel's messenger says. He rises up, or he stands. He flees in fear. He runs into the wilderness and then finally to Horeb, the mountain of God. At Horeb, he has a beautiful encounter with God in the faint whisper of the wind. It is here, at Horeb, that Elijah gets commissioned to find Elisha and anoint him in his place, to replace him so to speak. Reading through the account, all within a matter of what seems like moments Elijah is no longer powerfully moving forward with God's voice but is also in need of being replaced by another who will faithfully be attentive to the preoccupation that God imparts.

Let's unpack some of what just happened. Ahab and Jezebel are in council, and out of that meeting, Jezebel's desires find their way to Elijah. The problem is not that Ahab and Jezebel are in council. They are clearly seen as enemies here in the life of Elijah. The enemy and all of his desires will usually be stirred up against those who seek to be consumed by God's voice and consistently cultivate an obedience to it.

The problem is not found with Ahab and Jezebel and their council meeting. The problem is not found with the fact that Jezebel has messengers seeking to inform Elijah of her desires. The problem is not even found in the fact that Jezebel's message actually makes it to Elijah, that he receives and knows what the enemy thinks about him and is intending to accomplish in his life. None of these are the real issues. The real issue is found with what Elijah does with this other voice in his life. Again, the issue is not that Elijah receives the message. The problem is not at all found in the fact that Jezebel's voice has been moved to Elijah—it is that Elijah has been moved by Jezebel's voice.

Let's work through the progression that takes place in Elijah's heart and life. Elijah receives word about Jezebel's intentions. He processes Jezebel's desires in his heart. He stands. He is overcome by fear. He runs. This is the issue. Up until this point in Elijah's life he has only been moved by one voice. Until now, there has only seemed to be one dominating influence in Elijah's heart. That is, again, until now.

Elijah is now standing before the word of Jezebel. In his introduction in the biblical narrative we find him saying that there is a God before which he stands. Things have changed. There has been a shift in preoccupation. He has become fixed upon the voice of the enemy. The voice of the enemy has occupied his heart. Elijah is now being moved by Jezebel's voice. He is totally overcome by fear. He is now a man being motivated and animated by another presence and voice than the one of the God that he has come to know over his life.

Please do not miss this. When Elijah's preoccupation changes, so does everything about him. He ultimately ends up forfeiting his purpose in God because of the adjustment in what he is preoccupied with. When his preoccupation changes, he is now standing, or responding, to the wrong voice. When his preoccupation changes, he gets filled with fear. When his preoccupation shifts, he begins running from his purpose. When his preoccupation is altered, his prayer changes. He is now praying for God to end his life.

And then, after God comes to him in the whisper of the wind, someone else must now replace Elijah. Why? This seems extreme, doesn't it? For Elijah's responsibility, God couldn't have a man that was more impressed with the enemy's voice than His. He couldn't have a man that would yield to the influence of another voice above the voice that Elijah knew to be God's.

God couldn't have a man that was more impressed with the enemy's voice than His.

Everything about the way that Elijah prayed changed when the preoccupations of his heart changed. The prayer that came across his lips was radically altered when what filled his heart was radically altered. The direction of his life shifted when what moved his heart shifted. Elijah's lips and life were influenced when he chose to be influenced by Jezebel's desires rather than the God before whom he had learned to stand. All of Elijah's motivations and animation were radically altered when the preoccupations of his heart were disrupted. This is no small deal. This isn't just some side issue that we should easily and casually dismiss as if this only pertains to a specific man in a specific story.

Being consistent in the diligence to enter into His rest will deal directly with maintaining the preoccupations of your heart. Maintaining rest will directly affect your motivations. Maintaining rest will equally and directly affect what animates you. Let us be reminded and challenged by the life of Elijah that much can be won or lost depending on the way that we choose to manage and preserve the preoccupations of our heart.

Being consistent in the diligence to enter into His rest will deal directly with maintaining the preoccupations of your heart.

This is where the issue of Elijah's life falls into our conversation on rest and prayer. It so easily could become your life. It so easily could become you. Distracted by the voice of the enemy. Losing the preoccupation of your heart. Entertaining in prayer conversations that you should not even be having. Losing your sense of purpose in God, or begging God for audibles and alternative outcomes because of the pressure you experience.

This isn't how it's supposed to go. This isn't the way that God desires it to go. The Holy Spirit within you jealously longs to keep your attention fixed. The Holy Spirit within you longs to keep you centered on Jesus, focused on the word of the Lord, and resilient in pursuing what God has for you. This is the way.

CHAPTER 3
MOTIVATION

In this chapter we will discuss the motivations of the heart. Motivation is an interesting thing and that is why we will take time to discuss the implications of it in your life. To understand motivation, you could say that it is kind of like an energy that moves you to do something. Motivation provides a kind of fuel in your interior life to make things happen. The motivations of the heart are unique, because they don't explain what you are doing; they inform us of the why. The why reveals to us not how you are moving, or even what you may be moving toward, but again, the motivations of the heart give understanding as to what it is that is actually moving you, yet again, the why.

The why in your life is an incredibly difficult, yet necessary, thing to identify at times. However difficult it may be to process through the years of influence in your heart, it is a well-rewarded journey if you are able to arrive at the destination of what actually is in your heart that is moving you, motivating you, to speak and move the way that you do. There is a powerful desire within you, whether positive or negative, that is moving you. This desire is the energy, or motivation, that we are discussing.

The presence of the Lord helps to bring proper exposure to what is in our hearts.

It is important that we cultivate a life that is totally consumed by God's presence, and our awareness of that presence. For it is here, in the presence of the Lord, that all of the attitudes of our hearts are laid bare before the eyes of the One to whom we must give account. We must give account for what is in our hearts. It is in His presence that our hearts get sifted. His presence and His Word become the tools that powerfully sift through all of the imagery and the facades that we know how to hold up as a shield which keeps us from being exposed properly.

The presence of the Lord helps to bring proper exposure to what is in our hearts. It is the presence of the Lord and His Word that illuminate the inner man, shining a bright light into the enclosed spaces and places that otherwise go on as off limits to others.

The writer of Hebrews tells us that the Word of God is living and active and sharper than any two-edged sword and pierces as far as the division of soul and spirit, of both joints and marrow, and able to judge the thoughts and intentions of the heart.[10] Our hearts must be processed by the Word of God. The Word of God is powerful, and it is active. It is actively judging the thoughts of the heart. It is powerfully judging the intentions, or the attitudes, of the heart. It is to this thought that David writes, "Let the words of my mouth and the meditation of my heart be acceptable in your sight, O Lord, my rock and my Redeemer."[11]

It is important that the attitudes of the heart be pure, that they be innocent before the Lord. Distortion and disruption begin to creep into the heart when the attitudes of the heart go unchecked. We need our hearts continually processed by God's presence and His Word so that we know what the content is that is really contained within. For what is contained on the inside will eventually find itself to the outside, whether in word or in deed. If you want to deal with all that may be happening on the outside, meaning in activity or in language, you must first reveal what is influencing

---

[10] Heb 4:12, NASB
[11] Ps 19:14, NASB

the substance of what is found inside, dealing with the attitudes and intentions of the heart.

All of this has a direct connection to rest. The attitudes and thoughts of the heart influence rest. Many don't have rest because they aren't thinking such thoughts that would enable and empower rest within their heart. The beautiful simplicity found in a life of rest has been disrupted because there is a thought that has been sown which is negatively affecting the ease from within.

The ease from within easily ceases when the attitudes of the heart embrace a motivation that doesn't empower rest. The lack of rest many times experienced in the life of the believer is directly connected to thoughts from within that aren't compatible to a life lived in the beauty and ease that rest issues.

Luke chapter 10 gives us a story of two sisters, Mary and Martha. These two sisters are hosting Jesus, meaning Jesus has come to their house. Jesus has made an intentional choice to come to the place they reside in order to be with them. He has come to be with them. The vast difference in their approach to hosting Jesus illustrates our point here clearly and profoundly. We will begin with verse 38,

"Now as they were travelling along, He entered a village; and a woman named Martha welcomed Him into her home. She had a sister called Mary, who was seated at the Lord's feet, listening to His word. But Martha was distracted with all of her preparations; and she came up to Him and said, 'Lord, do you not care that my sister has left me to do all the serving alone? Then tell her to help me.' But the Lord answered and said to her, 'Martha, Martha, you are worried and bothered by so many things; but only one thing is necessary, for Mary has chosen the better part, which shall not be taken away from her.' "[12]

There is much to pull from these few short verses. The sisters in the story seem to provide us with two entirely different approaches to spending time with Jesus. Martha, according to Luke, is distracted with all of her preparations. She is consumed by things that she believes need to be done. There is a motivation within her to be impressive to Jesus by all of what she has within her own power to accomplish, or make ready, for Him. She is busy working for Jesus and working very hard.

---

[12] Luke 10:38-42, NASB

Mary, however, has been taken up with an entirely different posture. Mary isn't consumed by all of what may be perceived as needing to be done. Mary's life is consumed with Jesus. She is beyond content to sit at His feet and gaze into His eyes. She is enjoying His presence and being thrilled by His every word.

Mary's satisfaction isn't found in what she is able to accomplish for Him, but rather whatever it is that He would wish to accomplish while with her. Mary has found her rest in simply being with Jesus and being attentive to His presence. According to Jesus, Mary has chosen the better part, and He has no desire whatsoever to take it from her or remove her from her current placement.

Martha, however, is motivated to do something for Jesus, and her motivation doesn't allow for Mary's lack of movement. Martha finds her rest in being able to accomplish "things" for Jesus. Martha seeks to produce rest in her life by her productivity. Martha's perspective of what rest is, or should be, is directly confronted by Mary's position of rest.

Martha goes as far as to question Jesus about His seemingly lack of proper perspective and concern to bring correction to her sister. She questions His concern for how hard she is working when held up and against the lack of work that her sister seems to be doing. Martha's productivity and desire to perform well are being challenged by Mary's contentment to just be.

Martha is working hard so she can rest. Martha is attempting to be pleasing to Jesus. She believes that His pleasure in her life is directly connected to the work she is able to accomplish for Him. She wants to enter rest, but because of her perspective it first requires work. She believes her invitation into rest **Work shouldn't be what creates rest in your life. Your work should be issued out of rest.** is achieved through the compiling of a worthy list of achievements that would warrant such an invitation in her direction.

However right she may feel she is by thinking this way, she is not, she is not right at all, and she will find out soon enough. Martha believes that work comes before rest, and this isn't how it's supposed to be. Martha is performing this way because her heart has become programmed this way: work before rest.

The desire to work tirelessly in hopes that we will find rest because of our accomplishments is completely backwards. We aren't to work so that we can then rest, but rather we are to find rest so that we can then work. Work shouldn't be what creates rest in your life. Your work should be issued out of rest.

We don't work so we can rest. Much of the world and culture, especially in the West, is structured this way. Many find themselves waking up in the morning and working tirelessly all day long, hoping to accomplish enough throughout the day that would enable them a proper reason to then rest. Work, work, work, and then hopefully some time somewhere to be able to rest.

It doesn't matter if the majority of our own experience, and all of what surrounds us, is structured this way. It also doesn't mean that it is fully aligned with God's desires or design. Yes, it's true. Even the beginning of creation and the cycle of life itself testify to this reality and its power. In the beginning, the day began with the evening.[13] The Bible tells us that there was evening and there was morning the first day. This was God's design, evening then morning. This is really important to take note of.

The first day began with evening and then went into morning. This is an interesting order. The order reveals God's desire. The day began with evening because it is God's design that our day, or our beginnings if you would, would start with our entering into rest. We enter into rest so that we can get up and work, and not the other way around.

---

[13] Gen 1:5, NASB

Life has been programmed to tell us otherwise, but the creation account itself testifies to God's desires by His design. God created it according to what He desired. He desired rest first, so evening came first. Evening came first, which means that man would've had to rest and then in the morning rise to work. Do you see it? It's really simple, and overwhelmingly beautiful.

All of your work should be issued out of a beautiful place of rest. Is this the way it is for you? Do you find yourself being able to find a real, deep, powerful, beautiful sense of rest outside of your ability to produce accomplishments? Or is your ability to rest directly tied into your level of productivity? This potentially becomes very dangerous and hazardous to our ability to sustain rest in our lives.

If your ability to rest is directly tied into your belief that productivity is what grants rest, then what do you do when you aren't being "productive?" What do you do when you don't have any accomplishments to rest in? How do you handle your issue of rest in times when there is nothing for you to point to in order to validate your desire for rest, or your desperate need of it? You can begin to see the issues that this type of thought process generates.

Martha's aggressive desire to be pleasing to Jesus by her level of effort and productivity produced an aggravation with another who didn't have their life set up in the same manner. However frustrated Martha might have been by Mary, it didn't make Jesus feel the same way. We need to see this, understand it, and be freed by it.

Just because you feel a certain way doesn't automatically mean that Jesus feels the same way too, or that He even agrees with the way that you feel. You can be really passionate about things at times and be completely wrong at the same time. Passion or zeal doesn't equal truth. Martha is bound because she believes Jesus should agree with her. Jesus wants to set her free by her coming into agreement with Him.

A lot of times the way gets corrupted because we seem to believe that all He is concerned with is the *what*.

How precious it is for our hearts to be set free from our own way and limited understanding at times of what really matters to Him. Our incorrect perceptions, in coming to Jesus and aligning our lives with His heart and the truth contained in Him, can be shattered so that we can see clearly.

It isn't that Jesus doesn't care, or that He isn't at all concerned with things getting done; that's foolish to think. He expects us to work. He expects us to be faithful. He expects us to lay our lives down in diligence, giving an excellent yes to Him for things He calls and empowers us to do. However, He expects them to happen a certain way. Again, it isn't just the *what* that is important, but equally it is the *way* that matters to His heart as well. A lot of times the *way* gets corrupted because we seem to believe that all He is concerned with is the *what*.

I have heard it put best this way, "We need Marys that know how to work, and not just Marthas that try to learn how to worship."[14] This statement contains the life of the situation we are discussing. It is powerful because it speaks to the default posture. Mary has a default posture of worship. She is content sitting at the feet of Jesus. There is no desire within her to become consumed with any other, or anything other, than Jesus. She is at rest. Because she is at rest, anything that she may do will be issued out of, or come from and be formed by, her place and heart posture of rest. Her work will flow from rest, and it will not try to accomplish it. This is the difference maker, and it is why we must be confronted and freed within our own thinking and hearts.

On the other hand, Martha, however, is busy. She is distracted. She is burdened by many things. Her performance mentality is in direct opposition to the

---

[14] Talk with David Popovici, via phone call (2016).

thing that she claims to desire. She cannot see nor understand that her aggravation welling up within because of her own idea of what rest is, and the posture others take in relation to it, is a direct assault on her ability to rest herself. Her heart is stirred negatively because of the embrace of the attitude of her heart. She works first and will attempt to find worship whenever her work is done. She is busy working so that she can rest.

Mary's understanding of who she is comes from her place of restful attentiveness at the feet of Jesus. Her identity is formed in the presence of Jesus and what He says about her. Mary has been found in Jesus. She has found rest in Jesus, and therefore is ready for whatever may issue out of that restfulness. Jesus applauds this and has no desire to change what He has found in Mary.

Martha's understanding of who she is comes from her burdensome attempt to be productive to produce Jesus' attention. Her identity comes from her productivity. Martha is formed by what her work says about her, and other opinions that align well with her perceived correct thought process. Martha has no rest, for she will not sit first so that any effort she gives can be issued from resting.

Let's take a couple of moments and bring all of this home, meaning to the front door of our hearts.

To say it again, the Word of God is living, active, and powerful. It is able to sift through our motivations and bring judgment to the thoughts of the heart. We need this. It is for our good, and our freedom.

If asked right now, do you know what is motivating you? Are you able to identify what thoughts are providing the necessary energy to live the way you're living? An easier way to ask may be this way, who do you identify with more in the story we just discussed? Mary? Martha? Mary, with her joyful contentment in Jesus, restfully loving Him

Come to Jesus, sit, and let Him remove every unnecessary weight. Let the joy of His presence free your heart from the prison of productivity.

and being attentive to Him in every way? Or, Martha, and her wearying desire to prove her love for Him by being as busy and productive for Him as possible?

Is there something within you that needs to be dealt with that is directly affecting your ability to rest? Is it a performance mentality that needs to be broken? Again, it isn't that we don't want to perform well, or live faithful, productive lives. We just don't want to be taken captive by a thought that Jesus will reject us if we don't have "things" that we have done for Him to take notice of.

If you find yourself in the place that Martha did there is hope. If you find yourself burdened by so many things, things that don't matter as much when held up against simply resting and being attentive to Him, come and rest. Come to Jesus, sit, and let Him remove every unnecessary weight. Let the joy of His presence free your heart from the prison of productivity. Find freedom in looking into His face. He will free you. He will define you.

All of the stuff doesn't define you. Your productivity doesn't define you. Jesus defines you. Jesus gives your life definition. Your identity was never meant to be wrapped up in your level of productivity, or the work itself that you have applied your life to. The issue of identity is one that we will tackle and seek to unpack in the next chapter. Let us continue, for there is much to say about this. It will do your heart good.

CHAPTER 4
IDENTITY

There are certain fundamental and foundational things that you must understand about your identity in Christ. You are a son, or a daughter. That position, or relationship, is not formed by anything that you have been able to accomplish by way of merit or effort. There is One that has gone before you. There is One that has died for you in order to make this a reality and establish it forever. Jesus, the Son, has made a way. Praise be to God forever!

Our identity in Christ must be formed by what He says about us. It is important that our identity gets formed by what Jesus has to say and not by what other people have to say. The world around you, sometimes even well-intentioned people, will attempt to form you by their own opinions of you. However accurate these may seem at times, they are ultimately skewed, because people have a tendency to label you or refer to you according to the things that you do or have done.

This isn't the approach that Jesus takes. This isn't the definition that comes to your life from God the Father. The world labels you by your activity, or lack thereof. God has determined and settled His thoughts about you before you were ever formed in your mother's womb.[15]

Jesus doesn't define you the way the world does. He isn't insistent on making you earn your place with Him. Your identity in Him isn't developed by what you are able to do in order to prove your place. Your productivity doesn't give you an approval for the placement of a son, or a daughter. This is all a gift. It is all by adoption. It is initiated and continually empowered by a love that is beyond what our human language can adequately describe as good, and it constantly runs from the heart of the Father in your direction.

You are loved, deeply, immeasurably. Not because of what you have done, or even will do, but simply because of who you are and the value that the Father has attached to your life as His creation, His son, His daughter. This is a value that you cannot outwork. You cannot mess it up bad enough. You cannot simply decide one day that you no longer agree with the value

---

[15] Jer 1:5, NASB

that the Father has spoken over you and into you; it is and will always be. It was never your choice to initiate.

God's desire for you placed value on your life that you will never be able to shake.

God's desire for you placed value on your life that you will never be able to shake.

It is important to talk about your value before we consider the issue of identity and the relationship all of this has to activity. Identity, meaning who the Father says you are and your relationship to Him from this standing. And, then activity, meaning anything that you may do or feel called to do with your life.

We must consider value first, so that we don't get lost in the way we move through the progression and attempt to believe that value is directly attached to anything other than what the Father says. It happens very easily. Many times, people get lost and locked up into thinking that they must perform well in order to be valuable. That may be the case with sports, business, and other relationships that we may form in life. However, your value with the Father isn't formed this way.

Consider this. Even at the very beginning, in the most basic way of understanding our salvation, when you were at your worst, Heaven gave up its best for you. When you didn't care, the concern and jealousy of the Father was so much towards you that He was willing to lay down the life of His only Son for you. When your heart was corrupted and ultimately wanted its own sinful way, the purest love and life the world has ever known came as a peace offering in order to restore what you didn't even understand was broken.

The Bible puts it this way, as Paul writes in Ephesians, "But now in Christ Jesus you who once were far off have been brought near by the blood of Jesus."[16] Paul tells us, "For by grace you have been saved through faith; and not that of yourselves, it is the gift of God; not as a result of works, so that no one may boast."[17] And then beautifully David writes in the psalms, "Truly my soul finds rest in God; my salvation comes from him."[18]

It is important to frame in the conversation correctly. Creating the correct frame through which the talk of identity can be seen is imperative to the way that we live. It is imperative to the way that we live because it deals directly with the preoccupation of the heart, the motivations that flow from the heart, and the rest, or lack thereof, that will be created by such an internal conversation.

With all of this to consider, we must look at Jesus. We must look at Jesus, because as always, He is our

---

[16] Eph 2:13, ESV
[17] Eph 2:8-9, NASB
[18] Ps 62:1, NIV

blueprint. In searching the life of Jesus, we come to a grand moment in His life and walk when He approaches the waters of baptism and is confronted there by a man named John. Their interaction is one of great importance in order to create a Jesus-centered context to our talk thus far. We will pick up the story in Matthew's gospel, the third chapter.

"Then Jesus arrived from Galilee at the Jordan coming to John, to be baptized by him. But John tried to prevent Him, saying, 'I have need to be baptized by You, and do You come to me?' But Jesus answered him saying, 'Permit it at this time; for in this way it is fitting for us to fulfill all righteousness.' Then he permitted Him. After being baptized, Jesus came up immediately from the water, and behold, the heavens were opened, and He saw the Spirit of God descending as a dove and lighting on Him, and behold, a voice out of the heavens said, 'This is My beloved Son, in whom I am well-pleased.' "[19]

Jesus comes to be baptized. He isn't coming because He is filled with sin and needs to be cleansed. He is

---

[19] Matt 3:13-17, NASB

coming to identify with those that He desires to set free. He knows who He is and so He is settled in His heart to perform such a task, knowing that it doesn't diminish in any way the way that His Father feels about Him. In fact, He is able to freely obey all things, for He knows in His heart that His action doesn't affect His identification.

Jesus is lowered into the waters. When He rises and His face breaks the plain of the water top, Matthew writes that the heavens are opened, and a dove descends to rest upon Him. The restful posture of the dove signifies the Father's restful delight in His Son whom He loves. Not only are the heavens opened and a dove descends, but a voice literally thunders in the earth from the heavens and begins to declare definition over the life of Jesus. Wow, praise God! What an incredibly influential moment, I am sure, for Jesus, and especially for all of the others that may have been onlookers that day.

We must understand that at this point in Jesus' life He hasn't really done a whole lot that the world would deem "worthy" of such an occasion. He honestly has lived out the majority of His life in hiddenness and obscurity. He has been faithful in His parents' house. He has been diligent in developing His craft in work. However, there haven't really been any milestone accomplishments in His life to warrant such a response from others, much less from the heavens.

At this point in Jesus' life there haven't been any miracles. There haven't been any powerful public messages that He has preached. Thus far He hasn't raised anyone from the dead. Up until now there hasn't been a single person that the Bible gives witness to of Him healing. Up until now, there isn't any specific performance items that we can glean from that has made Him worthy for the Father to be overwhelmingly pleased with Him. But this is exactly the point that we must grasp in our hearts. It is the exact issue that we must allow the Holy Spirit to bring freedom to our hearts with.

His attention and affection for you and towards you is not being held hostage waiting for the ransom to be paid by your payment of *works*.

There is a freedom that is enjoyed when you are free from feeling like you have to earn your Father's attention with your efforts. There is a beautiful rest that is experienced when you simply come into full understanding and agreement that His goodness is towards you, and that it is not a byproduct of your perceived productivity that you come to Him with as an offering for His affection. His attention and affection for you and towards you is not being held hostage waiting for the ransom to be paid by your payment of *works*.

You don't have to work in order to be loved. There is no greater amount of affection that needs to be earned. If He loved you at your worst and came running in your direction willing to lay down His very life as an offering in order to reveal to you the love that He has for you, what would make you think that would change now dependent on your level of effort?

I know that these are easy things to agree with as you are reading over them, but let's pause for a moment and consider if you are fully living in the freedom and rest of things that are being described. A few quick questions should help us dig a little deeper than the surface agreement that most times helps to shield off the potential confrontation that lies within the heart from stirring up a conversation such as this.

Who would you believe yourself to be without the activity that your life may be expressing right now? You may currently be living in the believed call that is on your life, or you may be in a season of contending with and for a dream that you know the Lord has given to you, but either way, who would you be separate from all of it?

Would you know who you were if you couldn't flow in the gift that God has placed upon your life? If you have some sort of public *ministry*, whether locally or traveling, would you know who you were if you never got to touch a microphone again? Who would you be if you didn't have the business? If you didn't have the position? What would you think of yourself if you were completely stripped down of all the working and activities of your life?

We so easily fall into a vicious cycle where our lives are completely identified, or labeled, by the thing that we do. It sounds like this, "Oh, so you're a mom." "You're a business owner." "You're a preacher, or a pastor." "You're gifted in this area, or that..." That is typically the way the conversation goes. I'm not saying that what you do is to be entirely rejected. It very well may be a valid part and an expression of something that God has put on your life, but that isn't the point. The point is this: Jesus didn't need to do something to feel loved or valuable. Do you?

Take a moment and seriously consider what is being asked. Do you need something happening in your life other than the love of the Father to feel loved or valuable? Is there something in you that has not yet found rest with knowing that you are deeply loved, entirely separate from any sort of work, function, activity, gift, ministry, etc.? If not, there is a disconnect with your heart fully realizing and embracing the goodness of God's love towards you.

Jesus didn't have to work to earn love. He was totally convinced of it. Because He was convinced **Your assignment** of His Father's love, He was free to work. This is the progression **doesn't determine** that we want. This is the way **your identity.** that it should be. We should be so altogether convinced of the Father's love towards us that it frees us to work joyfully. And the work that we apply our lives to then becomes a joyous expression of our devotion unto the Father that has so lavished His love upon us. The alternative is that we end up becoming slaves to a work in an attempt to find the freedom found in being a son.

When we work from being at rest in the Father's love, we can work in joy because we know our laboring is not to earn His affection. When we establish rest and freedom in our hearts first, and then fully give ourselves to whatever the Father may be saying or asking us to do, we don't have to labor in fear, constantly wondering if our achievements are going to be enough to grant us entrance into the place of His attention.

You want to be at rest in God and what He says about you so you can joyfully fulfill whatever responsibility He may give to you. You identify with and in Him, so you are free to fulfill whatever the assignment might be. Your assignment doesn't determine your identity. Your assignment doesn't diminish your identity. This is why Jesus was able to be baptized that day. He was secure in who He was.

You may say, "Well, that's great for Jesus, but what about for me?" There is a special section in Mark's gospel that I have always loved. It's found in chapter 3. We won't take much time here, but it is too good to simply not include. Let's look quickly to that chapter. It's just a couple of verses, beginning with verse 13, "Afterward, Jesus went up on a mountain and called the ones he wanted to go with him. And they came to him. Then he appointed twelve of them and called them his apostles. They were to accompany him, and he would send them out to preach, giving them authority to cast out demons."[20]

There is a beautiful progression found in these verses. I am not one for three steps and stuff like that, but there are three phases here that are fundamental for us. In fact, this is the beautiful progression that all of our lives should follow.

First, Jesus goes up the mountain and He directly calls to those that He wants to be with Him. Our first call is unto Jesus. The greatest call upon your life is to

The greatest call upon your life is to go and be with Jesus and to love Him with everything you have.

---

go and be with Jesus and to love Him with everything you have. This is life's greatest call, loving Jesus.

Second, it is there in the presence of Jesus and being with Him in the place of His desire that Jesus gives their life definition. He appointed them as apostles, there, in His presence. The definition of our lives must be found in the presence of Jesus. He has the power to define you. He reserves the right to define you. The One that created you holds the right to give you definition. We must respond to His call to come to Him, and in being with Him, allow Him to speak in and over our lives in a way that will give our lives a proper definition. There is something very powerful about knowing who you are, and it is that you simultaneously know who you are not.

Lastly, Jesus sends them out to preach and gives them authority to cast out demons. Jesus gave their lives direction. Jesus sent them out. He sent them. Not to be really repetitive, but it is worth noting that they didn't send themselves; He sent them. They didn't just get up and go themselves. After being with Him for a bit they didn't just determine what they wanted to do and then go for it. Too many just get up and go on their own without being sent by Jesus. They begin chasing down responsibilities, activities, and direction that never actually come from a moment of commissioning by Jesus.

This sounds so simple, but it is powerful. They came to Jesus. In His presence they were first found in Him. Then they found out who they were. Then they found out what they were supposed to do. Because of the love that Jesus had for them He called them to come and be with Him. In the place of loving Him and being with Him they learned who they were, by Him speaking it into their hearts and lives. Then, once clear of their love for Him and Him knowing that they knew who they were, He sent them out to be who He said they were. This is amazing and should provide a great deal of rest and freedom to our hearts.

Jesus cares that you know who you are. He is committed to calling you to Himself and speaking directly into your heart and life in ways that will shatter every lie that you ever believed. And not just the negative ones. We immediately only attribute lies to things that are negative and damaging when there are also seemingly positive things we have believed and embraced that are not really from Him, and therefore are wrong.

Jesus is committed to you knowing who you are and what you are to do, but you have to go to Him to find out all of that. You must answer His call to come and be with Him, and find His rest, which is finding His freedom. He wants you to be free. Free to love

Him. Free to know who you are and are not. Free to know what you are then to do.

Rest is directly connected to freedom, for when we are at rest our hearts become freed from the motivations and conversations that have resisted rest. Freedom is directly connected to love, because perfect love will always lead us into greater expressions of freedom, which means that rest is attached to love. The love of the Father should bring rest to your heart and empower you to live in greater freedom.

> **Rest is directly connected to freedom, for when we are at rest our hearts become freed from the motivations and conversations that have resisted rest.**

The goodness of this love is something we will discuss in the next chapter in greater detail. He is really good, and the goodness of His love is overwhelming!

CHAPTER 5
GOODNESS

When you say God is good, what exactly do you mean? Day to day we comment on a lot of different things and refer to them as good. For instance, pizza is good. I have seen movies that were good. I have heard music that I thought was good. There have been times spent with friends that I referred to as a good time. But is this what we mean when we refer to God being good? This can't be it.

Saying God is good seems to fall short when considering the enormity and vastness of God's goodness, and especially that goodness in our direction. The human language seems to fail in attempt to refer to the overwhelming reality of God that has come crashing into my heart and my life. God is good, yes, but simply stating that He is good doesn't seem to adequately describe the conviction that my heart has developed of what that goodness means or the impact it has truly had.

However far it may fall short, I think it is a must that we declare and celebrate that God is good. He is good. He is overwhelmingly good. He is beyond amazing, and so good, that simply saying He is good seems to not be enough. But, again, since we have determined there is a lack of other ways to comment, we will say it again; He is good.

God is overwhelmingly good. He is beyond amazing, and so good, that simply saying He is good seems to not be enough.

We must be convinced that God is good. Actually, we must be beyond convinced; we must be convicted of God's goodness. And not just God's goodness in general terms, but that goodness towards us, as referenced earlier, actually pointed towards us in an intentional way by God Himself. God is not just good, in general; He is good to me. This must be our conviction.

We must be convicted that God is going to be good to us. For if at any point we fail in our conviction that God desires to be good to us, we will begin to enter into conversations that lead our hearts astray. It is a necessity that we find an anchor in our hearts in the goodness of God and refuse to be entertained by any other thought or argument that life or others would want to bring us into that would try to convince us otherwise.

Psalm 27 reveals the heart of a man whose life has been completely wrecked by the goodness of God. David has experienced something in the person of God that has completely and utterly changed everything about the way he sees life and interacts with it. David has experienced God and he could never simply be the same again. There is something very real that has happened to David's heart after encountering the goodness of God, and we know that because the mouth will always overflow with what is in the heart.

David writes these beautiful words, "I would have lost heart, unless I had believed that I would see the goodness of the Lord in the land of the living."[21] He goes on to say, "Wait on the Lord; be of good courage, and He shall strengthen your heart; Wait, I say, on the Lord!"[22] These are the words flowing from a heart that has been overwhelmed by how good God is.

David's perspective has been shaped by a hope that what he believes about God's goodness will not fail him. These words are special all by themselves, but the context in which these words are being expressed have much more to tell us about just how convinced David was. David is writing from a place of great challenge.

---

[21] Ps 27:13, NKJV
[22] Ps 27:14, NKJV

And the real test of all that we claim to believe will be found during times of great adversity. Trial and pain have a way of testing and purifying even the purest of intentions and claims.

Trial and pain have a way of testing and purifying even the purest of intentions and claims.

David opens Psalm 27 by declaring how wonderful God is. He says things like, "The Lord is my light and my salvation, whom shall I fear? The Lord is the strength of my life, of whom shall I be afraid?"[23] These opening words are tremendous in their ability to lift the heart and head. However, things take a little bit of a turn in the next couple of verses, and this is exactly where we find our encouragement for putting down an anchor into the goodness of God.

In the next two verses David mentions five words that tell us that he is not necessarily having a good day. David chooses to unveil the troubles that currently surround him. There is trial that has pressed up against David, and in his writing he freely expresses what he seems to be going through. David says there are: evildoers, adversaries, enemies, a host, and war. These are not five words you would use to give description to a

---

[23] Ps 27:1, NKJV

good time. But David is not having a good time, and this is exactly our point.

"When evildoers came upon me to devour my flesh, my adversaries and my enemies, they stumbled and fell. Though a host encamp against me, my heart will not fear; though war rise against me, in spite of this I shall be confident."[24] David isn't having a good day. David isn't standing in what sounds like a good spot. There is nothing about the way that David is describing his current experience that would lead me to believe that He is good.

But in the midst of all that may seem to the common onlooker from the outside as something that is not good, David holds up right smack in the midst of it all and declares that there is something about God's goodness that has so overwhelmed his heart and life that he cannot deny it, and that has now become his hope and strength. David is standing in the midst of a bad situation and declaring that God is good. What? I don't understand. How could David make such a statement? I'm glad you asked.

David understands that he doesn't have to experience good in order to be convinced that God is good. David doesn't have to feel good in order to remain confident that God is good. David doesn't need a good

---

[24] Ps 27:2-3, NASB

day in order to stay consistent in his declaration that God is good. In fact, David has learned something in the experience of God's goodness that has settled him once and for all, and this is the testimony that is shaping the heartfelt expression in this psalm.

David has been overcome by how good God is and that is now the lens through which he sees his own life,

The final verdict for God's goodness is no longer the circumstantial evidence of my life. God is good, period, end of story.

those around him, and all that life may try to bring his way. God's goodness has completely reshaped the lens through which David's heart sees life and he will not be detoured. There is something about his God and how good He has been to him that has created a perspective that David refuses to shake. He will not let it go.

David has learned a beautiful truth. For those who have matured in their walk with God, or are seeking to mature, there is a beautiful secret that David's heart has become convinced of, and it is this: Even if I don't feel good, experience good, or see good happening, God is good all the time. A heart that has become convinced of God's goodness realizes that the character of God is no longer standing trial in my heart based off of what is happening in my life day to day.

Regardless of what is happening in David's life, God is good. It is settled. David's heart is settled. Everything that happens will be processed through God being good. It is a nonnegotiable. This is no longer an item that is up for debate. This case has been closed. Regardless of what happens, however troublesome or painful it may be, it will all be processed through the lens of God and His being good, all the time. The final verdict for God's goodness is no longer the circumstantial evidence of my life. God is good, period, end of story.

David is no longer going to accuse God depending on what the experience of his life is dealing him in any given day. David isn't going to allow the insecurities of his heart to win out in the argument of who God is. There is no longer a place to put God on the stand and try His character based off of something happening in David's life that he might not understand or agree with.

God is good, and that goodness is established eternally and transcends all the momentary experiences of our lives.

This is a slippery slope. It makes the situations of your life the ultimate determiner of how good God is. This type of processor requires your experience to be one that can be categorized as good in order to maintain your current belief that God is good. The problem here is that God's goodness hinges upon your own personal evaluation of how that should be defined, and this will never be sufficient. God is good, and that goodness is established eternally and transcends all the momentary experiences of our lives.

David has come to a clearing in his heart. We know this to be true because of what David says he is after. He doesn't pray for answers to any of the perceived issues that he is experiencing. He is clear. He is focused. He knows what he is after. His heart is set on seeking the face of his God. And his seeking of God's face isn't conditional on his life circumstance.

David is coming after God during a difficult time. He's not holding his devotion ransom with a demand for answers as a payment so that he can continue to seek God and be faithful. David has matured beyond this elementary idea. He will not be detoured by any of what he sees because of what he has experienced in God.

David has found a refuge in God that has eclipsed his perceived need for answers to his problems or solutions to his issues. David isn't praying about either of these things. David knows that what he has found in the goodness of God has far eclipsed all of these other lower-level ideals. These other things may seem good, especially in a moment where pain is being experienced, but there is only one thing that is really good, and that is God—this is what David wants.

Paul echoes this same sentiment in Philippians when he says, "Not that I speak from want, for I have learned to be content in whatever circumstances I am in. I know how to get along with humble means, and I also know how to live in prosperity; in any and every circumstance I have learned the secret of being filled and going hungry, both of having abundance and suffering need."[25] But of course these words would be incomplete without the climax, "I can do all things through Him who strengthens me."[26]

Your being consistent can affect consistent change no matter where you are or what may be happening to you.

Paul found the secret. Paul learned over time that it was Jesus that really did it. There was nothing outside of the experience of Jesus that was able to prove successful. In seasons of suffering and great hunger and need, it was Jesus. In seasons of great abundance, it was Jesus. Paul had found the radical middle.

Learning the secret that Paul learned will help you to develop consistency with the Lord over time, which in turn, will produce maturity. In your growing and

---

25 Phil 4:11-12, NASB
26 Phil 4:13, NASB

maturing, the goal is to become what affects change, and to no longer simply be tossed around by what may be changing around you. Your being consistent can affect consistent change no matter where you are or what may be happening to you.

Consistency regardless of context is an expression of maturity. Consistency regardless of context is an expression of maturity. This is what Paul is describing for us. It no longer matters what he is going through; he has learned how to remain consistent in all settings and seasons. Paul has matured beyond the immaturity that says certain things are not possible until the proper context is provided. Paul has become fixed. Paul's life of devotion is no longer dependent upon what he has. Paul's consistency in walking with the Lord is no longer regulated by what *season* he is in. Again, Paul has learned the secret.

Paul is revealing to us what influences him. This is really what it is about. He is no longer moved by what he has or where he is. He is moved, he is influenced, by the Who he sees and the Who he knows is with him. Part of maturity is choosing the right influence. Many times, maturity and consistency hinge upon being moved by the right influence.

There is a tempering of the heart that the good-ness of God brings. Being settled in God and in His being good disarms much of the energy that is spent from within the heart attempting to create arguments as to why these things should not be true. There is a lot of energy spent attempting to undermine what you claim you have believed and embraced as reality in your heart.

The heart is a tricky thing at times, and if you are not careful you will find yourself playing its games. But you don't have to, and that is what David and Paul are both telling us. Both David and Paul had walked with God and allowed the Holy Spirit in real life and in real time to bring them up and into a higher place than the temporal experience of the moment that so many times locks up our hearts as prisoners to reason based off of our own evaluation.

Too much of what you pray and how you pray is possibly predicated on the what you see or the how you feel day to day. Paul's secret teaches us that our hearts are actually able to be more stable than this. This action, the day-to-day tossing of our hearts, is not the heart's greatest place of performance.

We must fight to become more secure. We must be diligent to set down our anchor. His goodness is steadfast. Because His goodness is steadfast, we have such promises as peace that surpasses all understanding.[27]

---

[27] Phil 4:7, NASB

Joy that is unspeakable, full of glory, and otherworldly in nature.[28] Hope that is impenetrable.[29] How could we not become fixed over time, immovable, settled? This is our portion as people of the Spirit and followers of Jesus. And this is to be the place that we posture our hearts in the place of prayer.

At times there are things you won't understand. At times there will be pain and pressures that you won't be able to explain. However, this isn't really the point. The point is that there is a beautiful place from within it all that your heart can be free and be at rest. You can be at rest knowing that He is good. You can remain at rest knowing that regardless of what happens to you or around you nothing can change His being good, or His desire to be good to you.

Whether you believe it or not right now, those two things are actually incredible fuel to the fire of consistency in your life and walk with the Lord. Much of what you battle in your heart will find a landing place in clearing up one of, if not both of, those statements. Clearing up both of those statements will aid in your learning and being developed in the one thing that David sought and the secret that Paul learned. Your heart being anchored in the goodness of God is a big deal. Your heart learning the secret of the goodness of

---

28   1 Pet 1:8, NASB
29   Heb 6:19, NASB

God and the sufficiency of Him being all in your life is a big deal.

Life has a way of pushing the buttons in your heart that, at times, are connected to insecurities that are just waiting for the right or wrong thing to happen in life so they can flare up and preach to you why they have been right all along. Insecurities are tricky because we don't always recognize that we have them until something happens and they flare up within us. Insecurities are actually a big deal. Insecurities must be dealt with. In fact, Jesus wants to confront and evict insecurities. This is exactly what we will discuss in our next chapter. Let's move on.

Your heart learning the secret of the goodness of God and the sufficiency of Him being all in your life is a big deal.

CHAPTER 6
INSECURITY

Rest and insecurity are opponents. They could never work alongside one another, for at the heart of what they are, they oppose one another. You can't be at rest while catering to insecurity. And the opposite is equally true. You can't continue to cling to insecurity when you find the freedom that comes from real rest. Insecurity and rest are in direct conflict with one another. Finding real rest in God provides the necessary tools by the Spirit to deconstruct insecurities that have challenged true rest.

Insecurity is a funny thing, very deceiving at times. My reference to insecurity is not the easily identifiable type, like the way you feel when someone says they don't like the way you look in a certain outfit. Or, the feeling you get when someone makes a sly remark about your new hairstyle. These are too much out on the surface of the heart, and they are also easy to accept for the point that we are going to make here. For insecurity, we will dig a little deeper into the depth of the hidden places of the heart. We will dare to plunge into, once again, the place of the motivations, to see if the light we shine brings anything out of hiding.

Insecurity, or better, the state of being insecure, can be defined as being subject to fears, or doubts. Also, insecure can be defined as not secure; exposed or liable to risk, loss, or danger. And finally, not firmly or reliably placed or fastened. These are all great ways to give description and definition to insecurity. As you will see, insecurity is much more than just an uncomfortable surface feeling when discomfort or offense is experienced.

Insecurity is much like a cancer. It runs through the heart and eats away at it until it has completely consumed all of the space available. Insecurity is incredibly challenging and damaging to rest. Insecurity, if not dealt with, has brought about the demise of many a formidable opponent. In fact, insecurity, when overlooked and counted as insignificant, or even worse when justified, is undefeated.

We spent time in the last chapter developing the idea that God is good. It is such a wonderful truth that we will say it one more time here, God is good! He is good, and He loves you. The consideration of

His goodness must be embraced in order to understand the implications of the goodness of His love. The implications?

Yes, the implications, and once again, I'm glad you asked. There are very real implications to God's love. The goodness of God's love, or more simply put, because His love is so good, means that it has a purpose. There are very real intentions with which God loves. These are the implications we are speaking about. His love is

> **The activity of love towards us and within us is working to remove fear from our hearts and lives.**

not random, or misaligned. His love is very pointed, strategic, and determined. There is a purpose with which and towards which God loves.

First John tells us that perfect love casts out fear.[30] According to the description John gives us, we are able to understand that love, in its perfect sense, is actively working within us to intentionally cast out fear. The activity of love towards us and within us is working to remove fear from our hearts and lives. The implications of perfect love having its way in our hearts is to completely remove any trace of fear that may reside within.

---

[30] 1 John 4:18, NASB

When considering the love of God, we have to understand that it is perfect. The love of God is perfect. Because God's love is perfect it is directly opposed to fear. God's love is intentionally working to drive out fear. God's love is intentionally working to drive fear out of your heart and life because fear is the root cause of insecurity. All insecurity has its founding in fear. Another way to understand it would be, fear is the manufacturing plant of insecurity.

All insecurity has its founding in fear. Fear is the manufacturing plant of insecurity.

It is important to understand that love has implications. Otherwise we will misinterpret its operation whenever it is at work. Typically, when we say that we are doing good, what we mean is that we are in a place where we may not currently be experiencing pain, pressure, discomfort, inconvenience, or something of like manner. This is usually what I mean when someone asks how I am doing and I respond with, "Good." I say I am good because I have associated being good with being free from any one of these listed descriptions. But, what if the operation of perfect love actually puts you directly into confrontation with one of these? Is this something that you have even considered to be possible?

If I don't really understand the work of perfect love within my heart, again to absolutely evict any hint or trace of fear, then I may mistake what is actually happening in a moment of my life. I may think I am discerning what is happening, something that is painful, and may attribute its source and intention to something or someone other than God Himself. But what if God is intentionally and directly working me towards certain painful confrontations, because He is good?

God is good, and because He is good and He loves you, and the way that He loves you is perfect, He is lovingly, perfectly, working you towards confrontations with any area of your heart that is currently holding onto fear. The perfect love of God is working in you to confront your fears. God's love is trying to free you from being afraid. It must be this way.

It must be this way because if it were any other way it wouldn't line up with what John has written to us about the implication of love. It must be this way because perfect love drives out fear. Perfect love wants to remove fear, which always leads to freedom. With that said, another way to put it would be to say, perfect love leads to freedom. It has to. God wants you to be free. He wants you to be free, but also understands that fear is one of the greatest resistors to that freedom that He desires for you.

God must deal with insecurity. Insecurity is rooted in fear. Insecurity is the byproduct; fear is the source. Your fears are developing insecurities. Insecurities are not your main issues, or the thing with which your greatest struggle should lie. It is the fear that is feeding that said insecurity. Dealing with fear will free you from insecurity. God is against insecurity because it is empowered by fear. God is against fear because it is hindering your freedom. And, this much is very true, regardless of how free you may feel right now, you are not as free as you could be. Thus, here comes the perfect love of God!

Areas of my heart grow in insecurity when I choose to trust in something or someone other than Jesus.

Insecurity, as we began with, can be defined as something that is unstable. It is unstable because it isn't secure, and anything that isn't secure is insecure. It is important that we identify that anything that does not have its rooting and bearings in the person of Jesus is insecure. It is insecure because Jesus alone is the only one and thing that is secure, and secure eternally. He is eternally the same, unchanged, He is fixed.

The way that Jesus causes us to become rooted in Him is to get us to respond to His love. Responding to the love of Jesus, by trust, develops faith. Trust becomes the hinge point of security. Trusting in Jesus brings freedom to the heart. As I trust Him more and more, He is able to free my heart more and more. It brings freedom to the heart because at times there are many other things that the heart wants to trust in.

Any anchor in my heart that I have put down into something or someone other than the person of Jesus is an insecurity. In any area of my heart and life that I have developed a trust that doesn't ultimately have its bearing in the person of Jesus is an insecurity. It is an insecurity because it is outside of Him, and He is the only thing eternally secure. It is an insecurity and it is temporary. It is temporary because it has an expiration date. It has an expiration date because it is outside of Him, and therefore it cannot last forever.

Perfect love is constantly attempting to prove to my heart that Jesus is enough.

At times God will have to challenge the things I have developed an anchor of dependency in to reveal the areas of my heart that have grown in insecurity. Areas of my heart grow in insecurity when I choose to trust in something or someone other than Jesus. This is the point. This is where perfect love is needed. Perfect love is constantly attempting to prove to my heart that Jesus is enough.

However, at times the heart finds greater pleasure in trusting in people and things that seem easier to control than Jesus. Things that are tangible, visible, more controllable, at times earn a greater place in our dependence for their immediate sense of being able to provide safety, comfort, satisfaction. But this doesn't mean that because they are able to speak this way in an immediate sense that what they speak is truth.

Fear makes us believe that there is something at stake to lose through surrender.

For all of this, God pours His love out in your direction, and one of the purposes of that love is to bring you to a confrontation with things you have chosen to trust in in a greater way than Him. Anything you are currently holding on to that makes you feel alive, gives you a sense of independence, or provides a false sense of comfort, outside of the person of Jesus, must be confronted. It must be confronted because it is leading you to greater expressions of insecurity and aiding in the development of your fears.

Anything that is restricting greater expressions of freedom must be seen as an enemy. Therefore, insecurity is an enemy to the level of freedom you experience and express. Insecurity wants to make you a prisoner to fear. Fear means that you become afraid. Afraid? Fear makes us believe that there is something at stake to lose through surrender. However, this is exactly where Jesus said we would find our life, and the greatest expression of our life. Jesus said that those who try to hold on to their life will lose it. But those who are willing to lose their life will find it.[31]

The love of God must lead you to confront what you think you need in order to live without Him. These are the things that must go. And not necessarily saying that you have to completely remove them from your life, but definitely speaking about the influence of them in your hearts. It sounds like this, "Abram, I need you to go and offer the life of your son, your only son, Isaac."[32] At the conclusion of it all Abram didn't have to actually lose Isaac. But he sure did have to be willing to walk all the way through it into a scary place that severed the influence of Isaac from the greater place of dependency that he had on God. This is the point.

If you can live free from the influence of it leading you astray, then you are okay. Astray, meaning into deeper places of dependency and insecurity. However, that isn't always the case. At times it will require a total severing. This is what I must be able to recognize or discern. Because again, if not, I will begin to fight

---

[31] Matt 16:25, NASB
[32] Gen 22:2, NASB

against the very thing that perfect love has come into my life to do.

I will begin to fight back, resist, and attempt to hold on to things and situations, because I will feel like things are being taken from me. That feeling of extreme loss in tenderly painful places will at times make me feel like I am dying. I will feel like I am dying because whatever is being touched, shaken, or taken must have provided some sort of life to me that God is trying to deal with in order to prove to my heart that He is more than enough and can be trusted in all areas.

You don't need to create other things to trust in so that you don't have to trust Jesus. Now, I know that sounds a little harsh when spoken so directly, but that is exactly what we have been talking about so far; that is the point we have been building. Some go to great lengths in order to create other anchors so that they can trust more in that than they do Jesus Himself.

Anything that your life is tethered to outside of having its bearing in Jesus must be confronted. Because God loves you the way that He does He will make it His mission to reveal the areas of your heart where this is necessary. Your career. Your ministry/gifting. Your bank accounts. Your relationships. Anything at all that is creating a resistance to dependency in Him as a real person, it must be confronted. It must be confronted so you can be free.

You won't totally be free until you know that you can live without certain things. If you can't live without it, you can't yet be fully trusted to live with it. You can't be fully trusted to live with it because of what will happen when it is asked for…you will believe you require it in order to live or feel fully alive and will then resist separating from it.

If you can't live without it, you can't yet be fully trusted to live with it.

Do you see the point? And the opposite is equally true. Anything that you can live free from you can be trusted with. The main influence in our hearts remains God and the goodness of His love.

All of this may seem to be a little heavy and tough to process. However, this is a dangerous process that greatly affects the heart and the rest God wants us to be able to enjoy. Our perspective of God's love has to be correct so that we are discerning what is truly happening in different moments and seasons. God's love is not just working within us to preserve our sense of happiness and comfort. God's love is actively working against our fears and seeking to reveal them so His love can totally destroy them from within us forever. This freedom is God's desire and plan for us. This freedom, from insecurities, affects everything.

Have you been able to find a place of rest during moments and seasons of perceived stripping? Have you been able to identify what exactly was happening to your heart and life in various moments of life and align the way you pray with the desires God was seeking to accomplish in those moments? Much of the time spent in prayer in these moments is spent in opposition to what God is actually attempting to accomplish. Again, rest is freedom that empowers innocence. While at rest we can be honest. An experience with perfect love helps us to be honest.

May it be our continual clinging to Jesus that weakens the strength of our ability to grip these other things we feel we need.

Once our hearts are stripped of all we sought to cling to outside of Jesus we can then truly and honestly cling to Him and Him alone. It isn't that these other things are not bad at times. They aren't, sometimes. In rest, we want to cling to Him. May it be our continual clinging to Jesus that weakens the strength of our ability to grip these other things we feel we need.

It is Him that your heart wants and needs. It is Him that makes the heart feel alive. It is Him that is our true security. It is Him alone that is our real comfort. Sometimes other things need to be rooted

out of our hearts in order for the truth of these statements to be beautifully experienced.

CHAPTER 7
WAITING

My soul waits in silence for God alone.[33]

I t is important that we discuss how rest in the place of prayer is affected by waiting on God. Out of the entire book, this chapter took me the most time, and that is fitting because this is the component that has affected my life in the greatest way. Waiting on God has broken me. Waiting on God has built me. Waiting on God has benefited my life tremendously, but possibly not in the way that you would anticipate making a reference like this would go.

Waiting on God has allowed me to clearly realize that God is all that I want. He is all that I need. And He is more than enough for me. Not what He does.

---

[33] Ps 62:1, NASB

Not what He gives. But, Him; Him as an all-consuming fire; Him as an overwhelming lover; Him as a comforter; Him as a shepherd. He is altogether lovely, and worth waiting for, on, and with.

Waiting on God is a gift. It has the power to reveal all of what is within that is not solely dependent on God alone. Waiting is the antidote to ambition.

Waiting on God is a gift, especially in the place of prayer. It is a gift from God because it has the power to reveal all of what is within that is not solely dependent on God alone. Waiting provides the necessary sifting to our hearts that is needed in order to know where our anchors are buried, and where our allegiances have been formed.

There is much happening in the place of waiting, most of which goes unseen, for it happens within the heart. The heart finds great exposure in the waiting, similar to photos that get developed in the dark. In the waiting, a lot becomes clear and becomes visible, most of which can only happen when you have provided the necessary space and time for exposure through waiting.

Waiting is the antidote to ambition. Waiting is the prescription for those whose hearts are hard bent on establishing their own way. The prideful attempt to lead God along in involvement for all of our own endeavors finds a beautiful confrontation in the place of waiting. For in the place of waiting we confront the pressures of life that attempt to forge our hearts in independence.

Much in life is attempting to make you your own god, for you to lead your own life by your own ways and your own wisdom, to be solely dependent on yourself and what you are able to do. This world has a wisdom that has excluded God from the equation and wants you to participate by its strategies and activities. Over time, this becomes a sickness to the heart. Waiting on God is the remedy that heals the heart of its woes that develop out of restlessness from not having decided to wait upon Him.

To those who choose to wait there are a handful of options. We can wait and let God lead. We can wait and then attempt to lead God. Whichever of the two you may choose is up to you, but know that there are only two pathways that arise out of waiting for the heart to select. There's not really a neutral option here. You can do your own thing, or you can do the thing that God leads you to do. The choice is yours.

Waiting in and of itself is a beautiful reality. For most, when waiting is mentioned, we think of sitting somewhere in isolation or solitude with the removal of external distraction or disturbance. However, this isn't all that is meant when waiting is referenced here. For you can remove all of the people, the noise, and the disturbances from the outside and still have a chaotic situation happening on the inside. Waiting is more about dependency than it is activity.

Waiting is more about dependency than it is activity.

Activity alone could never be the sole definition of waiting. For you could sit for hours in solitude and still arise never having formed a clinging to God in the depths of your heart. You can arise out of isolation and still seek the establishing of your own way by your own wisdom and power. Isolation doesn't promise dependency. Solitude has never guaranteed that one finds a genuine clinging to God and God alone. All of these are possible in the place of waiting, but they are not automatic byproducts.

Waiting provides the necessary crucible in order to be broken of our own self-will. For many it is the self-will that seeks to dominate in the place of their desires. They have not yet found the beautiful breaking that the Holy Spirit is able to bring. In waiting we find the necessary space that gets created for the Holy Spirit to bring us into a beautiful and powerful surrender that can alone be worked in us by God's desires. There is great breaking in the waiting. It is beautifully painful in every way. It is needed beyond comprehension.

The strength of our will that opposes God and His leadership must be broken. For as insurmountable a task as this may seem to some, waiting provides the necessary space and time in order to accomplish the task. In the place of waiting on God alone, the Holy Spirit is able to sift the heart. In the place of waiting, God is able to illuminate the areas of our heart that many times never get uncovered because of all of our busyness and activities. Please don't be fooled; not all activity is birthed out of waiting.

Not all activity is birthed out of waiting on God. Not all movement is infused with the life of the Spirit that is for those who have severed all other lifelines in prayer. There is much movement that happens in life that comes from the exact opposite place, no waiting. There are a lot of decisions that get made, a lot of situations that get created, a lot of initiatives that get birthed, and all from a place of not having waited upon God.

The strength of our will that opposes God and His leadership must be broken.

Many form things themselves and then present them to God. Many create or generate out of a lack of waiting and then beg and plead with God in order for Him to bless and prosper the things that they themselves have made. Abraham attempted this with Ishmael, remember?[34]

Some have just not slowed down long enough to understand what their efforts are being motivated by. Not every motivation of the heart is one that is from God. Much motivation comes from self-will, ambition, desperation, pride, brokenness, immaturity, and more. Prayer, and especially waiting on God in prayer, has the power to not only reveal what is moving us, but also make the necessary adjustments in the heart to where those other motivators are no longer governing the attitudes and actions of my life.

To those who don't know how to wait, or for those who haven't found the wonderful beauty and benefits of waiting, ambition, the strength of being self-willed, desperation, pride, the zealous drive of our own immaturity, and more become synonymous with faith. However, these aren't the same; they aren't the same at all. No matter how much effort and energy are put behind or into any of these categories they will never be the same as faith that arises out of waiting on God.

From the outside, when looking at people as they are moving, it is hard to determine who is actually being moved by God. Some have waited upon God and have taken the necessary time to free their hearts

---

[34] Gen 17:18, NASB

from the ideals and idols that motivate and animate, and they have broken into a clearing where they can confidently identify what faith looks like in a situation. Others are scrambling, moved by restlessness and a lack of confidence, attempting to make something happen or stick by their own effort. They are almost the same as throwing a dart in a dark room, hoping to find the light switch to see if you came close to a hidden target. This isn't how it should be. This could not possibly be the way that God has designed for things to go.

What does faith look like in a situation? That's a great question, and one that can only be answered and determined by a time of waiting upon God. For Moses, faith looked like standing still, with his staff held high before the Lord, to wait, watch, and see the salvation of the Lord.[35] However, Joshua, when lying on his face before the ark of the covenant (I am sure, attempting to go about it the same way that he had witnessed in the life of Moses, his leader and mentor for many years who knew from the Lord to be still and watch), heard the Lord say to him, "Get up off of your face and go and do what I have already commanded you to do."[36] I love that the prescription for what the posture of faith looked like was not the same. Rather

---

[35] Exo 14:13-14, NASB
[36] Joshua 7:10-12, NASB

than being systematic, it required a seeking, waiting, clinging, and then revealing of God's wisdom alone for both scenarios.

The action of faith must be determined in and through waiting. The personal accountability to the voice of God in the place of waiting must not be easily overlooked or discounted. God speaks and He desires to speak to you. He knows exactly what you are going through and what is needed for what you are facing.

Mimicking the movements of others will not always guarantee the outcomes of others.

The action taken by faith must be one that is initiated through dependency on God in the place of waiting, or else we may find ourselves mimicking the movements of others out of our lack of waiting for clarity from God Himself. Or we may find ourselves just simply trying to resort to things that we know have worked in prior moments and seasons of life. There can be moments where these behaviors may be right, but you will want them to be issued from God, through waiting, in order to determine if they are obedience or not.

Mimicking the movements of others will not always guarantee the outcomes of others, especially if God has not led you to behave in such a way. God may inspire you by what you see in others, but it should always press you back into God Himself, and not just into schemes and systematic movements that can be run through without dependency. Dependency is the goal. Dependency is what God is after. Dependency is formed in us in the place of waiting on God.

Not all movement is from and in rest. Many are moved by restlessness. It is their sense of desperation, or ambition, that is fueling all of their effort. Again, they haven't taken the necessary time to sit with God and allow the Holy Spirit to honestly sift their hearts. Time is a necessary ingredient in waiting. As funny as that sounds, because when you mention waiting it would almost automatically seem to imply that there is time involved. Yet, we must learn to wait beyond the boundaries of our current demands.

Most give God an ultimatum in the place of waiting. We have a specific slot that we have allotted for God to speak, to inspire, to reveal. But this isn't the same as waiting. This would be considered putting a temporary hold on our will. A temporary hold with a contingency that should God happen to intervene is not the same as truly waiting for God alone.

Waiting on God is not the same as giving God a time slot.

Waiting on God is not the same as giving God a time slot. Waiting on God allows God to be Lord over time. Giving God a time slot makes *you* Lord over time. Don't try to immediately create the argument that some situations have time-sensitive response requirements; we all know that. There is an issue much deeper than this. It is the control of time that the heart desires, and this is something that God and God alone deserves and has especially reserved for Himself. He works within time but remains Lord over it. Knowing that He is Lord over time allows us into waiting and empowers us in our waiting.

However difficult all of this may seem, it is still there, and we must be confronted by the beauty of David's words that flowed from his heart as he wrote this psalm—my soul waits in silence for God alone. David isn't waiting for answers; David is waiting for God. David isn't waiting for strategy. He isn't waiting for an immediate change in his circumstance. He isn't desirous of things; he will only be satisfied with having God.

This isn't to say that David couldn't use these other things, or that they wouldn't be a benefit. Sure, we wouldn't deny that. But he realizes that if he has God, the internal demand for all of these other things seems to lose its appeal. And, that in His time, God will deal with these other things His way.

David's heart has come into the profound realization that God alone is enough. God is enough because God Himself is all that is needed in order to be at rest. Rest is not a feeling; rest is a Person. Feelings are too temporary, and feelings also have expiration dates depending on what is fueling the feeling.

> **God is enough because God Himself is all that is needed in order to be at rest.**

Jesus' words must provoke our hearts into rest until we experience what it is that He promised, and that is, to give us rest by coming to Him. Rest is Jesus, and rest is in Jesus.

When entering into His rest we are able to experience rest, real rest. Rest that the world cannot offer, for its source is not found in the world. Waiting gives us the opportunity to realize all of what is producing restlessness in us. You don't believe it? Give it a shot and see all of the uprising within your heart that places a demand on you to move, to go on without Him, or to go on in an appearance that looks much like Him, yet is without the life issued out of rest in Him.

The bottom line is this: The strength of the will of the natural man must be brought into surrender to the loving rule of Jesus by the Holy Spirit. This is only made possible by the empowering presence of the Holy Spirit in our hearts and lives. Waiting gives permission to begin this work in our hearts. For in waiting we begin to understand what we are truly waiting for.

We aren't waiting on the Lord as if He is not with us. Oh, no, no, no, it is the exact opposite, my dear friend. We are waiting on the Lord so that we can realize how great of a reality it is that He is with us and that He truly is all that we need. For to the one that realizes his possession of Him through waiting, you already know that He is enough. He always has been, and He always will be.

So, then how long must we wait? Great question. To start, I would say as long as necessary to cross over to the other side of what has always moved you. Whatever time and space is necessary in order to produce something in you that will not move on without Him. The empowerment through waiting that would give you the ability to recognize the tug of your own will against the inspiration of His. This would be a good starting point. From here, He will satisfy. From here, He will lead. From here, He will empower. From here, He will be glorified.

CHAPTER 8
INTERCESSION

"Should we share with Abraham the things we are getting ready to do?[37]

It wouldn't seem to be a realistic goal to begin a conversation on intercession and then attempt to contain it to one chapter. However, there are a few things we can highlight about intercession that are made possible when our hearts are at rest in Him. Let's start here. Intercession can be defined as simply—a prayer to God on behalf of another. At times this can be self-initiated. It can be self-initiated by the desire within us for someone, something, or somewhere. Other times, intercession is not by self-initiation, but

---

37 Gen 18:17, NASB

rather by God's invitation. The second is what we will take a moment to unpack a little bit.

At rest, our joyful attentiveness can be fully given over to God and God alone. In this place, we can become more and more aware of His presence. In the enjoyment of His presence and the real delight of time spent with Him we can be absolved of all of our self-consciousness that so many times hinders real interaction with God. Self-consciousness is what would make you more aware of yourself, what you feel, or what you're going through than the reality of God's presence and His desires.

At rest, our joyful attentiveness can be fully given over to God and God alone.

Breaking free from being governed by self-consciousness is what begins to create a clear path for us to be able to receive what may be on God's heart. Not to say that this isn't possible any other way, but we are typically just so weighed down by our own self-consciousness that it eclipses this thought process altogether. Some that have always been controlled by self-consciousness have yet to realize that there could possibly be other things on God's heart that He desires to do than just rush in and tend to their comfort or current level of *happy* they are experiencing or not experiencing. God is more than a genie to fulfill our seemingly urgent wishes.

God has desires. This thought should pique our interest and provoke us into a prayerful place to investigate what may be on God's heart. Not only does God have desires, but He has always sought after a man or woman in the earth with which He could bare His heart and share those desires. This thought process is completely mind boggling. To think that the God that formed the entire universe, who has no beginning or end, is all powerful and all consuming, wants to share His heart with someone? And not just any someone, but with me? Yes, it is mind boggling, and it is very true, and should not be considered lightly or passively dismissed.

Throughout the Scriptures God's desire to bare His heart with His creation is clear. Ezekiel says, "I searched for a man among them who would build up the wall and stand in the gap before Me for the land, so that I would not destroy it; but I found no one."[38] Consider, in this situation God was looking for someone in the earth to stand in the gap, the meaning of taking up a place on behalf of another, and He was not able to find anyone for the task. There was not a single person whose attention God was able to capture that would

---

[38] Eze 22:30, NASB

share His burden. There was not one in the earth that would bear the heart of the Lord. Unbelievable.

In Genesis chapter 18 God appears to Abraham. Three visitors come to Abraham. Abraham and his wife host them. When the visitors get up and are prepared to leave, the Bible says that Abraham got up and walked with them. In this moment we find these words, "When the men got up to leave, they looked over to Sodom, and Abraham walked along with them to see them off. And the Lord said, 'Shall I hide from Abraham what I am about to do?' " Interesting, God seems to think He has found a man that He can invite into what is on His heart. God is ready to reveal the substance of the burden of His heart to a man. This is just crazy to think about, yet beautifully provoking at the same time.

Intercession is by invitation when God unveils His heart to you.

For those unfamiliar with the story, God shares with Abraham what He is about to do concerning the cities and peoples in a surrounding area. This revealing immediately draws Abraham into a beautiful place of prayer. Abraham begins to pray for the city and the people that God reveals are on His heart. He takes up the place of interceding because of what has been revealed to him. Prior to this interaction with God, Abraham was unaware of what was on God's heart.

Abraham found his invitation into intercession as God shared His heart with him. This is the point that we will highlight.

Intercession is by invitation when God unveils His heart to you. Our desire should be to steward the heart of the Lord well. God is searching. God is seeking after a man or a woman, someone who would take up the place of prayer with Him, contending for what is on His heart. This is a big deal, and it should be a big deal to us.

At times, it is so easy to be altogether unaware of what could possibly be bound up in the heart of the Lord because of all that's on my heart that I think is so urgent or pressing. I understand, there are legitimate times when the severity of what we may be facing requires a unique placement in our attention. This isn't what I am displacing. What I am displacing is the self-absorbed life that most live which completely overtakes them to where they aren't concerned with anything other than what pertains to them. It sounds like this—it must touch me in order for me to touch it in prayer. As sad as this may sound, it's true. And what is equally true is that God is still looking.

God is seeking after a man or a woman, someone who would take up the place of prayer with Him, contending for what is on His heart.

Our desire should be to steward the heart of the Lord. Stewarding the heart of the Lord in prayer means

There is a joyful unveiling in prayer where God will bear His heart and invite us into the carrying of His concerns and desires with Him.

that we are coming to God in the place of prayer to search out what may be on His heart. It means that we are communing with God in the place of prayer in order to bear His burden and tend to the concerns of His heart that He is longing to share. There is a sweet place of fellowship with God in the place of prayer where God cherishes the unveiling of His heart to His children. There is a joyful unveiling in prayer where God will bear His heart and invite us into the carrying of His concerns and desires with Him. This should be considered a great honor and a privilege, to steward the heart of the Lord.

All of this is not to say that we just completely forget about what we are going through. I agree that the things we face are real, they are pressing. However, what I am suggesting is that there is a higher place of concern. There is a grander frame of mind that we can become gripped by. Not that I forget what is happening to me, but because I have become gripped by what is on God's heart, I can become completely given over in prayer to the jealousy burning within me that longs to see the desires of His heart come to pass, even if it may seem as if I am not being attentive to what is happening to me.

What is burning in His heart becomes the burning of my heart. I don't ever want the influence of what is happening to me to be greater than the influence of His heart upon me. I want to be completely immersed in the desires of His heart. Being completely immersed in the desires of His heart is what disempowers the influence of things happening to me.

When God bears His heart to you, He is looking for a response. He isn't only sharing to inform you, but to invite you. Will you take up the place of secret prayer to steward the heart of the Lord? This is intercession. This is the response of a life that has caught a glimpse of what is on His heart and cannot simply live another day without jealously joining into the burden of the Lord in prayer.

> **Being completely immersed in the desires of His heart is what disempowers the influence of things happening to me.**

When we are at rest, we can be open to and intercede for what is on God's heart. Rest provides the necessary posture of the heart for the things that are on God's heart to be revealed to us. This is very different than interceding from a lack of rest, interceding for things that are being birthed out of restlessness. Much prayer, and intense prayer, happens out of restlessness. People trying to prove a point. People wearying themselves in prayer for things that God has never said. People attempting to exhaust themselves in prayer for matters that didn't initiate in God's heart. The struggle to wrestle in prayer for things that God never invited us to join Him in prayer about. All of what is born out of restlessness will never produce rest.

All of what is born from restlessness will never produce rest.

There is something else that is vitally important for the point we are establishing here, and it is this—Abraham didn't know what he needed to be in prayer about until he encountered God. It was in the place of presence that Abraham found out what he was to fill his prayer life with. Presence produced intercession. Or, to say it again this way, it was in the place of God's presence that Abraham found his invitation to intercession. Abraham knew what to set his face in prayer to by setting his face up against God Himself. This point cannot be discounted.

Abraham was interceding because he was looking at God. He wasn't looking at other people. He was completely caught up with God, and for that God caught him up in prayer with what was on His heart. This is the way it should happen. Presence should produce intercession. Intercession should be birthed out of presence. We should find our assignments for intercession out of the place of encounter, the place of encountering God's presence. Becoming aware of what is on God's heart should cause us to become aware of what to be taken up with in prayer.

Too many times we come running into His presence with things we want to intercede about. The only problem with this is that sometimes the things we are carrying are birthed out of incorrect motives—competition, ambition, prideful uncrucified desires, anger, insecurity, etc. Some don't realize they are interceding for God to *bless* something or *do* something that wasn't birthed in Him, out of His desires. And then some don't even know how to identify the difference.

Becoming aware of what is on God's heart should cause us to become aware of what to be taken up with in prayer.

We need to get into God's presence and completely let Him unravel our hearts. We need our hearts unraveled so we can find freedom in prayer. We need freedom in prayer so our lives are not all entangled by incorrect perceptions and motivations. We need freedom in prayer to be able to steward the heart of the Lord. Only when my heart is free can I steward God's heart sincerely. Sincerely means without manipulation, rest being a freedom that empowers innocence. Innocence means there is no manipulation.

This sounds really simple, yet it is impossible without the work of the Holy Spirit within us. We need the Spirit to set us free. Would you give the Holy Spirit permission to sift your heart? The prize always outweighs the pain. Keep going. There is a beautiful joy in rest, a joy unspeakable in His presence that has set our hearts and lives totally free to be attentive to Him. This is our pursuit. This is our promised inheritance. Then, may we take up the honor of intercession, "Your Kingdom come, Your will be done!"

CHAPTER 9
IN JOY, ENJOY

For a life in and by the Spirit, joy is not an option. Joy is not an option to those who have given themselves in complete surrender to this wonderful Jesus—it is a great promise. In fact, joy is inseparable from Jesus, because Jesus embodies joy eternally. Part of the very makeup of Jesus, embedded into His DNA, if you would, is joy. And when Jesus shares Himself with you, all of who and what He is gets revealed and imparted. So, when you come to Jesus you come to joy. This cannot be overemphasized.

You mustn't underestimate the dynamic power of real joy when it comes flooding into your soul like a violent tsunami. It is inexplicably delightful and wholly transformative in nature. We must say real joy because many times joy gets confused with its counterfeit, happy. To make the difference clear, happy is more connected to a mood, and joy is connected to a state of being.

It is important to make the distinction between joy and happy clear so we understand what it is that we are to contend for. **Joy is an eternal quality because Jesus embodies joy.** Happy is an emotion that is found in moments. Moments can be greatly influenced, and are in most cases, by circumstantial evidence. Circumstantial evidence deals with what is happening to me in any given moment.

When something good happens, I may feel or become happy. On the opposite end of this truth is its counterpart. When something bad happens to me, my sense of being happy may leave or diminish greatly. Happiness can be directly dependent on my situation and the results thereof. This fluctuating tendency of happy is what makes our pursuit of happy, or the attempt to lay an anchor into the hope of happy, so dangerous. It is dangerous because happy is temporary. It is temporary because it is dependent on how things are going, and how those things are going to make me feel. Happy is a feeling, and feelings have a tendency to be very fickle.

Joy on the other hand is an eternal quality. Joy is eternal because Jesus embodies joy. Anything that Jesus embodies, that is part of His character, His very being, must be eternal. It must be eternal because He is the same yesterday, today, and forever.[39] It must be eternal because we know He is unchanging, He is exactly what He is. And joy is part of what He is. And because joy is part of what He is, joy is what He gives and makes to come alive in us when He takes up residency in our hearts and lives. Joy is unavoidable when we are given over to a life of the Spirit.

Joy is very different than happy because joy is not dependent on a certain circumstantial outcome. Joy, because it is an eternal quality, doesn't have its rooting in this life or the results thereof—it has its bearings in Jesus. Joy isn't concerned with what is happening to me, because it understands its place and power within me. Joy isn't moved by what moves happiness. Joy isn't detoured by what voids my sense of happy. Joy is immovable, it is forever settled. What a powerful thought, and the implications of such a truth are very powerful as well for those of us who are in Christ.

Paul wrote it this way in Philippians, "Not that I speak from want, for I have learned to be content in whatever circumstances I am. I know how to get along with humble means, and I also know how to live in prosperity; in any and every circumstance I have

---

[39]   Heb 13:8, NASB

learned the secret of being filled and going hungry, both of having abundance and suffering need. I can do all things through Christ who strengthens me."[40]

In Paul's estimation, life was no longer simply about what was happening "to him." But rather than what was happening to him, Paul understood the powerful truth that there was something happening "in him." It is Christ who gives me strength. We must begin to see and understand joy is strength. Nehemiah told the people of his day that the joy of the Lord would be their strength.[41] Joy is a strong power within helping to form our lives into the image of Jesus, because once again, Jesus is full of joy.

Joy must be seen as a strength so that the operation of joy can begin to cripple the natural desire to be happy. Please don't misunderstand what I am saying here. Joy makes you happy. But you can also be happy and not have joy. The two are not the same. Just because you experience one doesn't automatically mean you have the other. If there is one side we want to contend for, it is joy. And this is what Paul is communicating to us in Philippians.

Paul has realized that joy in the experience of Jesus has the ability to disarm the influence of our lives, always desperately needing to create moments that

---

[40] Phil 4:11-13, NASB
[41] Neh 8:10, NASB

make us feel happy. These moments, and these scenarios, actually lose their appeal when we experience real joy. Real joy frees us to no longer be governed by the

Joy frees you from the prison of temporary emotional highs and lows.

feeling of what may be happening to us in a specific situation. When you have real joy, you are no longer a captive to the emotions of any situation you face.

Joy frees you from the prison of temporary emotional highs and lows. This is critically important in the place of prayer. Why? As always, I'm glad you asked. When my heart has found rest in God, and I am truly free to be joyful, which is to be full of joy, I have found one of the secrets to cultivating consistency.

Consistency in prayer must not be shaped by what is happening to you, but rather the One that you are continually coming to. Not consistency as in just the act of spending time in prayer, but rather consistency in the content of prayer. When we are not consistently coming to Jesus, too much of what we pray can be dominated by other things that we see and feel other than Him. Coming to Jesus is what keeps us consistent. Paul understood the secret; it is Christ in me. This wonderful Jesus, and the desire for Him, has now eclipsed all other longings of my heart. I only want Him.

To be only after Jesus means that He has become everything to you. Jesus is what is valued and cherished above all things. Jesus is your greatest obsession and your ultimate satisfaction. He is the fascination of your heart and life and unto Him you have given everything, because He has become everything to you. This sounds wonderful, I do agree, and we want it to be true and as authentic as possible.

When Jesus becomes your prayer, you are no longer so much consumed with praying your way into specific outcomes.

Jesus is everything. Yes! Amen! Glory to God! Which means that I am after Him and my prayer has become Him. My prayer has become Him, what? He is my greatest desire. To know Him, and all of what that may mean in every season of life. Like Paul penned so beautifully, whether experiencing lack or abundance, I have apprehended the secret, something greater than either extreme, and it is Jesus! The joy of Jesus and knowing Him intimately, deeply, and powerfully has become so much greater to me than the perceived accomplishment of a specific outcome.

When Jesus becomes your prayer, you are no longer so much consumed with praying your way into specific outcomes. Many try to pray their way out of things. Others are desperately trying to pray their way into things. The real joy is found in praying our lives into total surrender and complete satisfaction in Jesus. This is where real rest is found. Rest is found when He is everything, because the impulses and the influences that demand our attention and efforts lose the power of their grip. We are loosed and freed to be joyfully found in Him. This is the hinge upon which real joy can be experienced in a way that permeates your entire life and being.

I am not saying that what we go through or the desires we have aren't important. I am just saying that they aren't as important as Him becoming everything. To refer again to Paul's words, I have found the secret in all things, and it is Jesus. When I am going through trial, persecution, weapons formed against me, it is Jesus. When I am experiencing misunderstanding, a lack of clarity, no natural answers for what is in front of me, it is Jesus. When betrayal, lack, and confusion seem to abound, it is Jesus.

Real joy is found in praying our lives into total surrender and complete satisfaction in Jesus.

He is the secret in the midst of what may look and feel like these painful processes and places. And the opposite end of the spectrum is equally true; when I am experiencing mountaintop highs, it is Jesus. When I am going through celebration for breakthroughs and answers to prayer, it is Jesus. When my life seems to be in a space where God has given me rest from my enemies on every side, it is Jesus. It is Jesus in the perceived lows, and Jesus in the experienced highs. It is Jesus, all the time, this is the secret.

Let's put some of this into different words. Jesus must become better than the dream that you carry. Jesus must become more to you than the call on your life. Jesus must become sweeter than the ministry that you are in or that you desire. Jesus has to be more overwhelming than the business you are leading, involved in, or dreaming about beginning.

Are you getting what I'm after here? So much of our time and life gets wrapped up and into simply going after much that doesn't matter as much as Him. So much energy. So much attention. So much effort. All in an attempt to satisfy and bring rest to the heart. Hear me please—only Jesus brings rest and satisfaction to the heart. And once you have found true rest and satisfaction, you will then be ready to steward these other things with Him, especially in the place of prayer.

Many people don't enjoy Jesus and they don't enjoy prayer. And most are definitely not praying in joy. The idea and the practice have lost their appeal because there are so many other things that it has become about. It has become about answers. It has become about revelation. It has become about ambitious intercession. It has become about a tremendous amount of work and effort that seem to be pointed in a godly direction.

However, in the midst of all of this *stuff*, we have lost the simple, sweet, satisfaction of only Jesus. The joy of Jesus has been lost because of all that Jesus is able to do or provide. The enjoyment of Jesus gets lost in the shuffle of all of our other concerns. Our hearts become so easily cluttered. Our hearts become so easily distracted. Our hearts, and the gaze thereof, so easily become dimmed to the beauty of His face when the bright shining demands of life and its entanglements seem to glisten roundabout.

In joy you must enjoy. Your life of prayer, faithfully walking with and loving Jesus, must be one that is saturated in joy so that you, in joy, can enjoy. Don't settle for less. Radically press your life into Him until this is your testimony. And I don't say radically as if to imply that you will need to shout your vocal cords out or stay up all through the night pounding your fist and head against the floor. No, no, no, in fact it is quite contrary to that.

Simply find a quiet place to get away with Him. Gather your heart as best as you know how. Look to Him. Look unto Him. Give Him all of your attention.

In this place, as honest as you know how to be, give Him everything. Sit, open your heart, rest, resist the temptation to think you are waiting for something when in fact you are already waiting with someone.

Let the precious work of the Holy Spirit sift through the desires and demands of your heart until you begin to feel the chords of burdens loosed.

It is Him. It will always be Him. He comes like a flood, rushing to those to look unto Him. In this place, let His joy begin to flood your heart, defeating all of the dissatisfied desires that have been attached to things, people, and outcomes. Let it all go. Let the precious work of the Holy Spirit sift through the desires and demands of your heart until you begin to feel the chords of burdens loosed. Let Him lighten your heart, fill you with Himself, and set you free to be joyful!

Looking unto Jesus... author & finisher of my faith. Ha, it starts w/ You Lord ends w/ You & everything in between. You truly are all in all. My all, my everything. You made yourself nothing, to give me everything! Thank You Yourself! Phil 2

CHAPTER 10
HONESTY

Rest allows you to be honest. One of the ways that honesty can be defined is as a freedom from deceit or fraud; truthfulness, sincerity. Your heart desperately needs the freedom to be honest. It may take a little bit of processing in order to figure out what the honesty of your heart is crying out for, but it is a task that the Holy Spirit is more than up for, and powerfully able to perform.

The desires of your heart matter to God. They matter to God because He is the One that formed you. He is the One that said yes to you. He knew you before you were in your mother's womb. He has a plan for your life. He has a dream that He dreams about you. His dream for you is what He wants to fill your heart with. He longs for you to dream with Him as He has been dreaming about you.

When I say *your* desires, what I mean is this: your heart becoming intertwined with God's heart. Your heart being intertwined with God's heart is what enables the content that is in God's heart for you to become what is in your heart for you. Your life finds its greatest satisfaction and expression when you are dreaming the dream that God is dreaming about you.

Your life finds its greatest satisfaction and expression when you are dreaming the dream that God is dreaming about you.

The psalmist wrote it this way, in speaking of Jesus, "I take joy in doing your will, My God, for your instructions are written on my heart."[42] I know this may sound somewhat difficult to understand, but it isn't intended to be. Actually, it's intended to be really simple and plain. In fact, sometimes it's so simple that it often gets overlooked because of its plainness and simplicity.

Our hearts become so convoluted by life. The demands. The opinions of others. The experiences we have and things we come to believe along the way that shape the person we are today all play a key role in what we are currently dreaming about. Being honest is about recapturing the dream that burns in your heart.

---

[42] Ps 40:8, NLT

Being honest is about digging through all of the stuff that so many times buries deep within the dream that we once knew. Being honest is about inventorying all of the clutter of our hearts that resists our attention from being given over to it because of what other things in life seem to be crowding all around.

We can begin by asking a few questions. Let's start by asking questions that deal with people and how they affect what you may be dreaming. What would you do if you weren't worried about what people thought? What I mean is, if you weren't worried about impressing a certain crowd? If you weren't worried about finding a place of belonging in a specific circle? If you didn't care about proving a point to people and their opinions about it wouldn't matter?

What if you weren't concerned with disappointing someone because you weren't doing what they thought you should be doing? If you didn't have in mind the things that people have always told you about what you should be doing? You have to see how all of these potentially affect what you call your dream. All of these influencers have a powerful effect on the way you dream and what you are actually willing to pursue.

What would you do if you weren't afraid? What I mean here is this, if you weren't afraid that someone would tell you that it isn't important enough? What if you weren't afraid that it wouldn't be a lofty enough goal for your life? What if you were no longer afraid that you weren't going to be good enough? That you would somewhere along the way fail and have to deal with the consequences of investing time, money, resources, into something that you didn't actually feel qualified enough to pull off?

All of these different questions, and there are many, many more if we wanted to continue to take the time to survey them out, powerfully inform our hearts as to what we feel we should be dreaming.

Let's make it really practical for a moment. It would sound like this—maybe you've always prayed about how you were going to be in business because you come from a family of people that have always been in business. Maybe your prayer has always been that you were going to be involved in "ministry" somehow, fulfilling a certain role or capacity, because you thought that if you didn't your life wouldn't really count to God.

Maybe you have always prayed about joining the military because you are a part of a family lineage of people that have seen it as your duty to do so. I think you can understand the type of thought process that we are attempting to highlight by the examples given thus far.

The point we must see is that maybe we have been pursuing something that we don't even honestly want or desire but have just never been free enough to be able to see it that way. Possibly our heart has never been free enough, meaning at rest and satisfied enough without anything other than Him, to honestly and freely come to

The world is waiting for those who are fulfilling and fully manifesting God's desires to the world around them.

such conclusions regardless of the perceived consequences that historically have always motivated our hearts' pursuit down certain paths. The point is to come to an opening in our heart where we are able to take inventory and identify what has been happening, or is happening, and be satisfied enough in Him to be honest about it.

All of creation is waiting for the revealing of the sons of God.[43] Those who are joyfully surrendered to the Father. Those who, by the Spirit, are free from the worldly entanglements that seem to bind so many. The world is waiting for those who are fulfilling and fully manifesting God's desires to the world around them. Those not bound by carnal ambitions, but radically transformed by and infused with the burning of their Father's heart. A people that are possessed by God's dream, and His dream for their life. A people who will

---

[43] Rom 8:19, NASB

not and cannot be satisfied by anything other than Him. A people given over to His Kingdom and seeing it come on the earth as it is in Heaven. A people found in His rest, and diligently praying for His will to be done.

I pray that you find yourself deeply embedded into His rest. I pray that it transforms everything about how you love Him. It is my hope and my great desire that in rest you become unrecognizable, for as free as you may think you are right now, you aren't as free as you can be. Dear friend, be overwhelmingly loved by Him. Love Him in return. Never look back. It only gets better from here. It's time to pray...

Michael Dow

Michael Dow and his wife, Anna, have been married for thirteen years and they have four children together. Their family resides in Orlando, FL where they lead a growing group of house churches called The Father's House. He is the cofounder and president of Burning Ones, an international ministry team helping people all over the world experience the love and power of Jesus and live more passionately devoted to Him. Michael is the author of several books, including *Fasting: Rediscovering the Ancient Pathways.* Michael holds an undergraduate degree in theology from Southeastern University in Lakeland, FL and travels the world preaching the Gospel with powerful signs and wonders following into gatherings of all kinds.

STAY CONNECTED TO MICHAEL DOW

 @michaeldow

/michaelsdow

@michaeldow

BECOME A PARTNER

BURNING ONES IS HELPING PEOPLE AROUND THE WORLD
EXPERIENCE THE LOVE AND POWER OF JESUS AND LIVE
PASSIONATELY DEVOTED TO HIM.

FOR MORE INFORMATION ON BECOMING A PARTNER
SCAN THE QR CODE BELOW OR VISIT:

BURNINGONES.ORG/DONATE

DOWNLOAD THE BURNING ONES APP
STAY UP TO DATE WITH ALL BURNING ONES NEWS

In the app you will have access to messages, worship,
news and updates, the Bible, livestream events, and much more.

RESOURCES

FOR OTHER BOOKS, RESOURCES, AND MERCHANDISE
SCAN THE QR CODE BELOW TO VISIT THE
BURNING ONES ONLINE STORE.

CONNECT

CONNECT WITH BURNING ONES

@_burningones

@burningonesinternational

www.youtube.com/burningones

Info@BurningOnes.org

Burning Ones
PO Box 772610
Orlando, FL 32877